THE GREAT PUMPKIN COOKBOOK

A Harvest of LIBBY'S Favorite Recipes

A Rutledge Book

All recipes in this book were developed and tested by Home Economists in Libby's Home Economics & Consumer Service Department.

JoAnn J. Shurpit, *Director, Home Economics & Consumer Services*
Carol Parik, *Manager, Test Kitchen*
Betty Heinlen, *Home Economist*
Jeannine Angio, *Home Economist*

Photography: Dick Jones
Illustrations: Joan Blume
Public Relations Coordinator: Vivian Manuel

Cover Recipes (clockwise from front left): *Cool Harvest Moon Soup, Festive Double Decker Salad, Great Pumpkin Cookies, Peace Pipe Pie With Caramelized Almonds, LIBBY'S Famous Pumpkin Pie, Peanut Brittle 'N Pumpkin Parfaits, Carol's Cranberry Nut Bread, Pumpkin-Eater Doughnuts, Stuffed Green Peppers Ranchero, Pumpkin Pasta and Scrumptous Pumpkin Date Torte*

Library of Congress Cataloging in Publication Data
Main entry under title:

The Great pumpkin cookbook.

Includes index.
1. Cookery (Pumpkin)   I. Libby, McNeill & Libby, Inc.
TX803.P93G74   1984   641.6'562.   84-11541
ISBN 0-87469-044-7

Printed in the United States of America
First Printing

CONTENTS

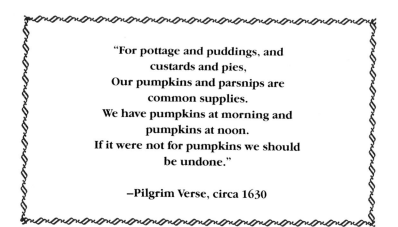

> "For pottage and puddings, and
> custards and pies,
> Our pumpkins and parsnips are
> common supplies.
> We have pumpkins at morning and
> pumpkins at noon.
> If it were not for pumpkins we should
> be undone."
>
> –Pilgrim Verse, circa 1630

THE LIBBY'S PUMPKIN STORY

When the Pilgrims finally made port in Plymouth, they found a cold, unwelcoming land. But, thanks to local Indians, there were some pleasant surprises too: the yellow grain called maize, wild cranberries from the marshes, tart-sweet beach plums, various beans and nuts, and a golden fruit of the vine, the pumpkin.

Pumpkins had been grown and used in Europe and some other parts of the world long before the Pilgrims set sail. The word "pumpkin" came to us by way of the old French *pompion,* in turn derived from the Greek *pepōn* meaning "cooked by the sun."

American Indians ate pumpkin both boiled and baked, and made soup of it at harvest time. They also cut pumpkins into rings and hung them to dry in the sun, then stored them for winter. Some of the dried pumpkin was ground into meal and used to make breads and puddings, adding variety to their maize-based diet. The Plymouth Thanksgiving festival lasted nearly a week, and a large party of friendly Indians, including the chief,

4

Massasoit, shared in the festivities. The bill of fare for this first Thanksgiving feast has not been handed down to us, but it probably included turkeys, ducks and geese. The Indians furnished venison and other game. The vegetables appear to have been the same as those now used at Thanksgiving: native squash and pumpkin.

In New England, the earliest pumpkin pies were made by cutting off a slice from the top of the fruit, taking out the seeds and filling the cavity with milk, spices, and honey or maple syrup or molasses, whichever was available. Then the top slice was replaced and the whole pumpkin baked.

This method certainly changed dramatically when, in 1929, Libby, McNeill & Libby, Inc., introduced solid pack canned pumpkin. The Dickinson variety was used—superior in flavor, richly golden in color, creamy smooth in texture—and is still the only pumpkin Libby packs. Now home cooks could easily make consistently excellent pumpkin dishes. Moreover, this wonderful pumpkin could be enjoyed all year around, not just at harvest time. Innovative cooks began to think of more and still more ways to use this versatile ingredient in dishes that ranged all through the meal: velvety soups; unusual main dishes and side dishes; golden, fine-crumb cakes; cookies plump with nuts and raisins; wonderful changes on the familiar pumpkin pie theme; and dozens more. Happily, they discovered that pumpkin goes well with just about everything, standing deliciously by itself or as a perfect foil for a wide variety of flavors.

Perhaps mothers don't admonish their children, "Eat your pumpkin—it's good for you!", but Libby says it and says it proudly. Pumpkin is an excellent source of many nutrients. It is rich in Vitamin A, and also contains good values of iron, potassium and Vitamin C, as well as other nutrients necessary to the well-being of the body. It is low in calories, sodium and fat—good news for those who must watch their diet.

For example, one cup of LIBBY'S Solid Pack Pumpkin—with only 80 calories—provides 600% of the U.S. Recommended Daily Allowance for Vitamin A, 20% of the iron and 15% of the Vitamin C—plus other nutrients such as magnesium, phosphorus, riboflavin, calcium, protein, niacin and thiamin—with only 10 mg. of sodium and a trace (1 gram) of fat. And that cup of solid pack pumpkin also provides a whopping 470 mg. of potassium.

Nothing is added to LIBBY'S Solid Pack Pumpkin—no sugar or salt, no artificial flavorings, colorings or preservatives. Pumpkin is the only ingredient. The amounts of nutrients, vitamins and minerals listed on the can label are those that occur in the pumpkin naturally. Libby adds nothing, keeping the product as close to "natural home-grown" as it can be. So you can enjoy pumpkin in dozens of ways, secure in the knowledge that your personal favorites are as nutritious as they are delectable.

Pumpkin has a subtle taste. When used as an ingredient in baked goods, pumpkin adds extra moistness and rich golden color. In savory dishes, pumpkin melts the flavorful ingredients beautifully.

Small wonder that just about everyone loves pumpkin, no matter how it is served. If you have confined your family enjoyment of this golden ingredient to pies, you will want to broaden your horizons with the many creative recipes in this book, all using pumpkin in pleasurable, unexpected ways. Whether you have mastered the culinary arts—or are only a sometimes-cook—there are sure to be many dishes here that will gain instant acceptance and that you will want to serve over and over again. And you can try them all with confidence because every recipe in this book has been kitchen-tested by Libby, McNeill and Libby, Inc., to assure you of successful results in your own kitchen.

LIBBY'S FAMOUS PUMPKIN PIE AND PIE TOPPERS . . . BETTERING THE BEST

America's choice with glorious toppings galore

What signals the arrival of autumn? Is it for you, as it is for so many home cooks all over the country, the first homemade pumpkin pie of the season? Pumpkin pie is a long-standing American tradition. And since 1950, when **LIBBY'S Famous** Pumpkin Pie recipe first appeared on the Libby canned pumpkin labels, American home cooks have known that they can bake a consistently superior pumpkin pie with Libby's help. For more than 15 years, nutritional information has appeared on the label as well. The easy recipe has been updated to reflect changing baking habits, particularly the use of pie crust mixes and ready-prepared crusts. So you can be confident of producing a flavorful, custard-smooth dessert, pie after pie after handsome, spicy-sweet pie.

LIBBY'S Famous Pumpkin Pie

When you've been America's favorite for over 30 years, you've got to be good. More than good, this smooth, gently spicy, pumpkin pie is perfect!

2 eggs, slightly beaten
1 can (16 oz.) LIBBY'S Solid Pack Pumpkin
¾ cup sugar
½ teaspoon salt
1 teaspoon ground cinnamon
½ teaspoon ground ginger
¼ teaspoon ground cloves
1 can (12-13 oz.) evaporated milk or 1½ cups half and half
1 9-inch unbaked homemade pie shell with high fluted edge

Preheat oven to 425°F. Combine filling ingredients in order given; pour into pie shell. Bake 15 minutes. Reduce temperature to 350°F. Bake an additional 45 minutes or until knife inserted near center comes out clean. Cool; garnish, if desired, with whipped topping. Yields one 9-inch pie.

VARIATION:

If regular 9-inch frozen pie shells are substituted, recipe fills two. Slightly thaw pie shells while combining other ingredients. Pour filling into pie shells. Preheat oven and cookie sheet to 375°F. Bake on cookie sheet 45 minutes or until pies test done with a knife as noted above.

VARIATION:

If a deep dish 9-inch frozen pie shell is substituted, recipe fills one. Let shell thaw 20 minutes, then recrimp edge to stand ½-inch above rim. Pour filling into pie shell. Preheat oven and cookie sheet to 375°F. Bake on cookie sheet 70 minutes or until pie tests done as noted above.

Pie Toppers

For a delightful change of pace, crown your next pumpkin pie with one of these delectable toppings.

Peanut Crunch Topping
Crush enough peanut brittle with a rolling pin to make 1 cup; sprinkle over cooled pumpkin pie before serving.

Zesty Orange Glaze

In saucepan, combine ½ cup sugar and 2 tablespoons cornstarch; mix well. Gradually add ¾ cup orange juice. Cook until clear and thickened, stirring occasionally. Add 2 tablespoons thinly shredded orange peel. Cool slightly. Spoon over cooled pumpkin pie. Chill until serving time.

Golden Walnut Crunch Topping

Mix 1 cup coarsely chopped walnuts with ⅔ cup firmly packed brown sugar. Drizzle with 3 tablespoons melted butter or margarine; stir until mixture is uniformly moistened. Sprinkle over cooled pumpkin pie. Broil about 5 inches from heat for 1 to 2 minutes or until topping is bubbly. Cool; garnish with whipped topping and extra walnut halves, if desired.

Coconut Cloud Meringue

Beat 3 egg whites with ½ teaspoon vanilla extract and ¼ teaspoon cream of tartar until soft peaks form. Gradually add 6 tablespoons sugar, beating until stiff peaks form. Spread over hot pumpkin pie, carefully sealing meringue to edge of pastry. Sprinkle with 2 tablespoons shredded coconut. Bake at 350°F 7 to 10 minutes or until golden brown. Cool.

Dairy Cream Topping

Serve cooled pumpkin pie topped with dairy sour cream, plain or sweetened to taste.

Crunchy Pecan Topping

In small bowl, combine 1 cup chopped pecans, ⅔ cup firmly packed brown sugar and 3 tablespoons melted butter or margarine. Sprinkle mixture over baked, cooled pumpkin pie. Broil, about 5 inches from heat, 2 minutes or until topping is bubbly. Cool. Garnish, if desired, with whipped topping or whipped cream and additional pecans.

Honey Blossom Topping

Drizzle a thin stream of orange blossom or clover honey over cooled pumpkin pie.

Zesty Orange Glaze, Dairy Cream Topping, Golden Walnut Topping, Almond Cream Topping, Coconut Cloud Meringue

Coconut Cream Topping

In small bowl, beat 2 packages (3 oz. each) softened cream cheese with ¼ cup sugar and 1 egg yolk until smooth. Carefully spread over pumpkin pie which has been baked only half of total required baking time. Sprinkle with ⅓ cup flaked coconut. Continue baking remaining time or until center is set. Cool. Garnish with toasted slivered almonds.

Sesame Cream Garnish

Spread 1 tablespoon sesame seeds in shallow pan. Toast at 400°F about 3 minutes or until nicely browned. Fold sesame seeds, 2 tablespoons powdered sugar and 1 teaspoon rum flavoring into 2 cups whipped cream. Spoon over cooled pumpkin pie.

Almond Cream Topping

Combine 2 cups whipped topping with 1 tablespoon almond flavored liqueur; mix well. Chill. Spoon over cooled pumpkin pie. Top with toasted sliced natural almonds.

Honey Whipped Cream Topping

Fold 1½ tablespoons honey into 2 cups whipped cream. Spoon over cooled pumpkin pie.

Holiday Mincemeat Topping

Combine 1 cup prepared mincemeat with 2 tablespoons orange juice. Spoon over cooled pumpkin pie.

Caramel Peanut Glaze

In small skillet, combine 3 tablespoons firmly packed brown sugar, 2 tablespoons butter or margarine and 1 tablespoon cream or milk. Cook, stirring constantly, until mixture melts and bubbles for 1 minute. Stir in ½ cup coarsely chopped peanuts. Spoon over baked cooled 9-inch pumpkin pie.

Creamy Orange Topping

Fold 3 tablespoons powdered sugar and 2 teaspoons grated orange peel into 2 cups whipped cream. Spoon over top of cooled pumpkin pie, leaving a border of pumpkin showing. Garnish with 1 cup drained Mandarin orange segments.

APPETIZERS/SOUPS . . .
BRIGHT BEGINNINGS

*Tasty appetizers, soups both hot and cold, all
made with pumpkin*

Whatever is served first, whether a palate-pleasing appetizer
or a tempting soup, sets the tone for a whole meal. And when
these starters must stand alone as party appetizers, or soups
served as the center of a light lunch or supper, it's even more
important that these foods are pleasing to the eye and deeply
satisfying in flavor. That's where pumpkin comes in. Because it
partners so perfectly with a wide variety of other flavors,
pumpkin is the ideal starting point for substantial, perk-up-the-
appetite finger foods, both hot and cold, to serve when you
entertain. And when soup is on the menu—deep-down good,
hot soup that hits the spot on winter days, or delicate, chilled
soup that entices lagging hot-weather
appetites—canned pumpkin is on
hand to help you turn out the
perfect dish to suit the
occasion.

Hearty Golden Soup

With the help of a crisp salad and fragrant homemade bread, this soup, hearty with mushrooms and rice, becomes a satisfying meal.

½ cup chopped onion
½ cup chopped celery
2 tablespoons butter or margarine
2 cups chicken broth
2 cups sliced mushrooms
½ cup rice, uncooked
½ teaspoon salt
½ teaspoon tarragon
1 can (16 oz.) LIBBY'S Solid Pack Pumpkin
2 cups half and half
¼ cup dry sherry

In medium saucepan, sauté onion and celery in butter. Add broth, mushrooms, rice and seasonings. Bring to boil. Cover; simmer 20 minutes or until rice is cooked. Stir in pumpkin; continue cooking 5 minutes. Stir in remaining ingredients; heat thoroughly. Yields 6 cups or 4 to 6 servings.

Creamy Garden Soup

To be served hot or cold, this light soup is based on chicken broth enriched with pumpkin and delightfully spice-and-onion flavored.

2 cups chopped onion
¾ cup green onion slices
¼ cup butter or margarine
3 cans (10¾ oz. each) chicken broth
1 can (16 oz.) LIBBY'S Solid Pack Pumpkin
¼ cup chopped parsley
1 bay leaf
½ teaspoon salt
½ teaspoon curry powder
¼ teaspoon ground nutmeg
⅛ teaspoon pepper
2 cups half and half

In large saucepan, sauté onion and green onion in butter. Stir in broth, pumpkin, parsley, bay leaf, salt, curry powder, nutmeg and pepper. Bring to boil. Reduce heat; simmer, uncovered, 15 minutes, stirring occasionally. Remove bay leaf. Transfer soup in 2 cup portions to blender container or food processor. Cover; blend at medium speed until smooth. Repeat with remaining soup. Return to saucepan; stir in half and half. Heat thoroughly. Yields 8 cups or 6 to 8 servings.

NOTE: Soup can be served chilled, if desired.

Hearty Golden Soup, Creamy Garden Soup, Sopa de Calabaza

Sopa de Calabaza

Cheddar cheese and pumpkin are the chief ingredients in this creamy, hot soup. Green chilies and cumin supply peppy seasoning.

2 tablespoons butter or margarine
1 cup chopped celery
½ cup chopped onion
2 cans (10¾ oz. each) chicken broth
1 can (16 oz.) LIBBY'S Solid Pack Pumpkin
2 tablespoons chopped green chilies

1½ teaspoons ground cumin
1 teaspoon salt
Dash pepper
2 eggs, slightly beaten
1 cup half and half
2 cups (8 oz.) shredded sharp cheddar cheese

In 3-quart saucepan, sauté celery and onion in butter. Add broth; bring to boil. Reduce heat to simmer. Add pumpkin, chilies and seasonings. Stir with a wire whisk until well-blended. Cover; simmer 10 minutes. Remove ½ cup pumpkin mixture, gradually add to eggs, stirring constantly. Gradually add egg mixture back into soup, stirring constantly. Cook over low heat 5 minutes. Add half and half and cheese; heat thoroughly. Do not boil. Garnish with coarsely chopped tomato; serve with corn chips, if desired. Yields 6 servings.

Pumpkins were very popular among American Indians long before Columbus landed. When the Spanish sailed down the Rio Grande, the Indians they met offered them pumpkin seeds as a gift of peace.

Cool Harvest Moon Soup

What's just right on a hot summer evening? A smooth, easy-make soup to tempt lagging appetites.

1½ cups boiling water
2 teaspoons instant chicken bouillon
1 can (10¾ oz.) condensed cream of chicken soup
½ cup LIBBY'S Solid Pack Pumpkin

¼ cup half and half
Dash celery salt
Dairy sour cream
Chopped chives

In blender container or food processor, dissolve bouillon in water; add soup, pumpkin, half and half and celery salt. Cover; blend thoroughly. Chill. Stir before serving. Garnish with sour cream thinned with additional half and half so it will float on soup. Sprinkle with chives. Yields 3½ cups or 4 servings.

NOTE: Soup can be prepared in bowl using a rotary beater or electric mixer.

Pumpkin Cheese Ball

Tangy smoked beef is the surprisingly perfect flavor partner for this handsome, pumpkin-shaped, cheddar-and-cream cheese appetizer spread.

1 package (8 oz.) cream cheese, softened
½ cup LIBBY'S Solid Pack Pumpkin
1 package (2.5 oz.) smoked sliced beef, chopped

2 cups (8 oz.) shredded sharp cheddar cheese
¼ cup crushed pineapple, well-drained
1 tablespoon chopped onion
Short celery stalk

Combine cream cheese and pumpkin, mixing until well-blended. Stir in beef, cheddar cheese, pineapple and onion; mix well. Chill at least 1 hour. Form into large ball. Score sides with knife to resemble pumpkin. Garnish with celery for stem. Serve with crackers. Yields about 2½ cups.

Pumpkin Party Dip

One of the great crowd-pleasers, this delicious pumpkin, orange marmalade and yogurt dip complements any piece of fresh fruit.

½ cup LIBBY'S Solid Pack Pumpkin
½ cup sweet orange marmalade
½ cup plain yogurt
¼ teaspoon ground cinnamon
⅛ teaspoon ground nutmeg
Dash ground cloves
½ cup whipping cream, whipped
⅓ cup coarsely chopped pecans
Apple slices, strawberries, orange sections, pineapple or banana chunks

In medium mixing bowl, combine pumpkin, marmalade, yogurt and spices; mix well. Fold whipped cream into pumpkin mixture. Spoon into serving dish. Chill. Before serving, top with nuts. Serve with assorted fruit dippers. Yields 2½ cups.

Bread Basket Dip

What could be more party-practical than a savory pumpkin and cheese medley served in its own warm 'n crispy edible bread basket?

1 8-inch diameter round French bread loaf
3 cups (12 oz.) shredded sharp cheddar cheese
1 package (8 oz.) cream cheese, softened
1 cup dairy sour cream
¾ cup LIBBY'S Solid Pack Pumpkin
½ cup green onion slices
½ cup chopped parsley
1 package (2.5 oz.) smoked sliced beef, chopped
1 tablespoon Worcestershire sauce
Dash hot pepper sauce
Vegetable dippers

Preheat oven to 300°F. Hollow out bread loaf leaving ½-inch shell. Cube bread; reserve. Combine cheddar cheese, cream cheese and sour cream, mixing until well-blended. Add pumpkin, green onion, parsley, beef, Worcestershire sauce and hot pepper sauce; mix well. Spoon mixture into hollowed loaf. Wrap in foil. Bake 2 hours. Serve with bread cubes and vegetable dippers. Yields 5 cups.

Heavenly Cocktail Balls

*Double pumpkin goodness here, in spicy miniature meatballs
and in tart, tangy pumpkin-and-apple juice sauce.*

1 pound ground beef	1 egg, slightly beaten
½ pound ground pork	2 teaspoons salt
1 cup quick or old fashioned	1 teaspoon ground allspice
oats, uncooked	¼ teaspoon pepper
¼ cup finely chopped onion	Pumpkin Sauce
½ cup LIBBY'S Solid Pack	
Pumpkin	

In large bowl, combine meat, oats and onion; mix well. Add
combined pumpkin, egg and spices; mix well. Chill 10 to 15
minutes. Preheat oven to 375°F. Roll mixture into 1-inch balls.
Place in ungreased 15½x10½-inch jelly roll pan. Bake 25 to 30
minutes. Remove immediately from pan. Serve with hot Pumpkin
Sauce. Yields about 6 dozen.

PUMPKIN SAUCE:

1 can (16 oz.) LIBBY'S Solid	1 teaspoon prepared
Pack Pumpkin	horseradish
1 cup apple juice	¼ teaspoon ground allspice
½ cup barbecue sauce	

In medium saucepan, combine ingredients; bring to boil. Reduce
heat; simmer 15 minutes, stirring occasionally. Serve in chafing
dish over hot meatballs. Yields 3 cups.

NOTE: Cooked, cooled meatballs may be tightly wrapped and
frozen, if desired. To serve, thaw in refrigerator. Combine with
sauce; heat thoroughly.

MICROWAVE:
Prepare meatballs as directed. Place in 11¾x7-inch baking dish.
Cook on High (100%) 4 to 5 minutes. Rearrange meatballs,
bringing balls from the outside of dish to the center. Cook on
High (100%) 4 to 5 minutes or until lightly browned. Let stand
2 minutes. In 2-quart casserole, combine Pumpkin Sauce ingredients. Cook on High (100%) 7 to 9 minutes or until thoroughly
heated, stirring after 4 minutes. Serve over hot meatballs.

BREADS/ROLLS/BREAKFAST . . . FRESH AND FANTASTIC

Fragrant breads and breakfast specialties, golden-rich with pumpkin

When the incomparable aroma of baking bread permeates the house and spills out into the neighborhood, all the great perfumes of France don't stand a chance in comparison. There is little as satisfying as fresh-made bread, rolls and sweet loaves, pancakes and waffles, and all the other baked treats. And when the family baker tries a different ingredient, one that expands the baking repertory and provides new taste pleasures, everyone benefits. With pumpkin as an ingredient, you can turn out bread and rolls that are splendidly fragrant, richly golden, with a wonderful texture and an unbeatable flavor. And pumpkin is a great show-off when combined with other favorite baking ingredients, such as fruit, nuts, cheese and spices.

Festive Pumpkin Ribbon Bread

Hidden in the center of this home-baked whole wheat loaf made with orange juice lies a silky ribbon of orange-peel-spiked cream cheese.

FILLING:

1 package (8 oz.) cream cheese, softened
2 tablespoons orange juice

1 teaspoon grated fresh orange peel or ½ teaspoon grated dried orange peel

Preheat oven to 350°F. Combine filling ingredients; mix until well-blended.

BREAD:

1 cup all-purpose flour
1 cup whole wheat flour
2 teaspoons baking powder
1 teaspoon salt
½ teaspoon baking soda
1 teaspoon ground cinnamon
½ teaspoon ground allspice or ground cloves

1 egg, slightly beaten
1 cup sugar
1 cup LIBBY'S Solid Pack Pumpkin
½ cup orange juice
¼ cup oil

Combine flours, baking powder, salt, baking soda and spices. Combine egg, sugar, pumpkin, orange juice and oil. Add dry ingredients, stirring until just moistened. Spread half of batter into greased and floured 9x5-inch loaf pan. Gently spread filling down center. Top with remaining batter, sealing in filling. Bake 65 to 70 minutes or until wooden pick inserted in center comes out clean. Cool 10 minutes; remove from pan. Cool completely. Yields 1 loaf.

VARIATION:

An additional 1 cup all-purpose flour may be substituted for whole wheat flour.

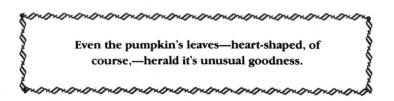

Even the pumpkin's leaves—heart-shaped, of course,—herald it's unusual goodness.

All Seasons Tea Bread with Creamy Cheese Spread

Pumpkin and zucchini for superior moistness, a whiff of cinnamon for zest—try this unique loaf sliced and spread with a creamy cheese mixture.

1 cup LIBBY'S Solid Pack Pumpkin	2 cups flour
1 cup grated zucchini	1 teaspoon baking soda
¾ cup sugar	½ teaspoon baking powder
2 eggs, slightly beaten	½ teaspoon ground cinnamon
¼ cup oil	¼ teaspoon salt
¼ cup butter or margarine, melted	½ cup chopped pecans or walnuts

Preheat oven to 350°F. In large bowl, combine pumpkin, zucchini, sugar, eggs, oil and butter; mix well. In separate bowl, combine flour, baking soda, baking powder, cinnamon and salt. Add dry ingredients to pumpkin mixture, mixing until just moistened. Stir in nuts. Spoon into well-greased 9x5-inch loaf pan. Bake 60 minutes or until wooden pick inserted in center comes out clean. Cool 10 minutes; remove from pan. Yields 1 loaf.

VARIATION:

Substitute grated carrot for zucchini.

CREAMY CHEESE SPREAD:

1 package (3 oz.) cream cheese, softened	3 tablespoons butter or margarine, softened

Combine ingredients; mix until well-blended. Spread between slices of All Seasons Tea Bread.

On prosperous farms just after the American Revolution, kitchen gardens produced a wide variety of fruits and vegetables. Pumpkins and squash were particularly esteemed because they, along with potatoes, could be stored in the root cellar for the winter.

23

Pumpkin-Go-Round Coffee Cake

Two richly aromatic yeast bread rings with flavorful pumpkin filling—great for a brunch, or serve one, freeze the other.

FILLING:

1 cup LIBBY'S Solid Pack Pumpkin	½ cup milk
	½ teaspoon ground cinnamon
½ cup sugar	¼ teaspoon ground ginger
1 package (3¾ oz.) instant butterscotch pudding mix	⅛ teaspoon ground cloves
	½ cup chopped nuts

In mixing bowl, combine all filling ingredients except nuts; beat 2 minutes. Add nuts; refrigerate.

DOUGH:

4 to 5 cups flour, divided	½ cup milk
½ cup sugar	½ cup water
1½ teaspoons salt	¼ cup butter
2 packages (¼ oz. each) active dry yeast	2 eggs

In large bowl, mix 1½ cups flour, sugar, salt and yeast. In saucepan, combine milk, water and butter; heat until liquids are warm (120-130°F). Add to dry ingredients; beat 2 minutes at medium speed, scraping bowl occasionally. Add eggs and ½ cup flour, or enough to make a thick batter; beat at high speed for 2 minutes. Stir in enough additional flour to make a stiff dough. On lightly floured surface, knead dough until smooth and elastic, about 8 to 10 minutes. Place in greased bowl, turning to grease top. Cover; let rise in warm place until double in volume, about 1 hour. Punch dough down; divide in half. Roll half the dough to a 20x7-inch rectangle. Spread with additional melted butter and half the filling. Roll up from wide side. Seal edges; shape into a ring on greased baking sheet with sealed edge down. Seal ends together firmly. Cut slits two-thirds through to center of ring at 1-inch intervals; turn each section on side, working quickly. Repeat with remaining dough and filling. Cover; let rise in warm place, until double in volume, about 1 hour. Preheat oven to 350°F. Bake 15 to 20 minutes. Remove from baking sheets; cool on wire racks. Yields 2 coffee cakes.

ICING:

2 cups powdered sugar	2 tablespoons milk

Combine powdered sugar and milk; mix well. Drizzle over cooled coffee cakes.

Pumpkin Raisin Muffins

Even the kids can put together packaged nut bread mix, pumpkin and raisins to make these easy-do, cinnamon-sugar-topped snacks.

1 package (16.1 oz.) nut bread mix	½ cup raisins
1½ cups LIBBY'S Pumpkin Pie Mix	1 egg, beaten
	1 tablespoon sugar
	½ teaspoon ground cinnamon

Preheat oven to 375°F. Grease bottom only or line medium-size muffin pans with liners. Combine nut bread mix, pumpkin pie mix, raisins and egg; mix until just moistened. Spoon into muffin pans, filling each cup ⅔ full. Sprinkle top of each muffin with combined sugar and cinnamon. Bake 20 to 25 minutes or until wooden pick inserted in center comes out clean. Cool 5 minutes; remove from pans. Yields 1 dozen.

MICROWAVE:

Prepare as directed. Place doubled paper baking cups in 6-ounce custard cups. Fill each cup half full. Sprinkle with cinnamon sugar mixture. Arrange six custard cups in ring in oven. Cook on High (100%) 3½ to 4½ minutes or until wooden pick inserted in center comes out clean. Repeat with remaining batter.

Easy Pumpkin Swirl Rolls

Start with refrigerated crescent rolls and add a tangy apricot filling for these coffee-time treats.

1 cup LIBBY'S Pumpkin Pie Mix	2 packages (8 oz. each) crescent rolls
½ cup chopped dried apricots	Sugar

Preheat oven to 350°F. In saucepan, combine pumpkin pie mix and apricots. Cook over low heat about 10 minutes or until thick. Cool. Separate crescent roll dough into four rectangles. On a surface lightly sprinkled with sugar, roll out each rectangle to 7x4-inches. Press to seal perforations. Divide pumpkin mixture evenly among rectangles. Spread mixture almost to edges. Roll dough from wide end. Place on cookie sheet; cover and refrigerate. When dough is firm enough to slice, about 10 minutes, cut into 1-inch slices. Arrange in two 9-inch buttered cake pans. Sprinkle lightly with additional sugar. Bake 25 minutes or until golden brown. Yields 10 to 12 servings.

Pumpkin Nut Bread

A long-time favorite, richly spiced and fragrant—make a large loaf for the family, mini-loaves for truly appreciated gifts.

2 cups flour
2 teaspoons baking powder
½ teaspoon baking soda
1 teaspoon salt
1 teaspoon ground cinnamon
½ teaspoon ground nutmeg
1 cup LIBBY'S Solid Pack Pumpkin

1 cup sugar
½ cup milk
2 eggs, slightly beaten
¼ cup butter or margarine, softened
1 cup chopped walnuts or pecans

Preheat oven to 350°F. Sift together first six ingredients. In mixing bowl, combine pumpkin, sugar, milk and eggs. Add dry ingredients and butter, mixing until just moistened. Stir in nuts. Spoon into well-greased 9x5-inch loaf pan. Bake 65 minutes or until wooden pick inserted in center comes out clean. Cool 10 minutes; remove from pan. Yields 1 loaf.

VARIATION:

For two mini-loaves, spread batter into two well-greased 7½x3¾-inch loaf pans. Bake 50 minutes.

VARIATION:

For two large loaves, use one can (16 oz.) LIBBY'S Solid Pack Pumpkin; double remaining ingredients.

> "Let no man make a jest at pumpkins," wrote one thankful settler in 1654, "for with this fruit the Lord was pleased to feed His people to their good content, till Corne and Cattel were increased."

Pumpkin Raisin Muffins, All Seasons Tea Bread

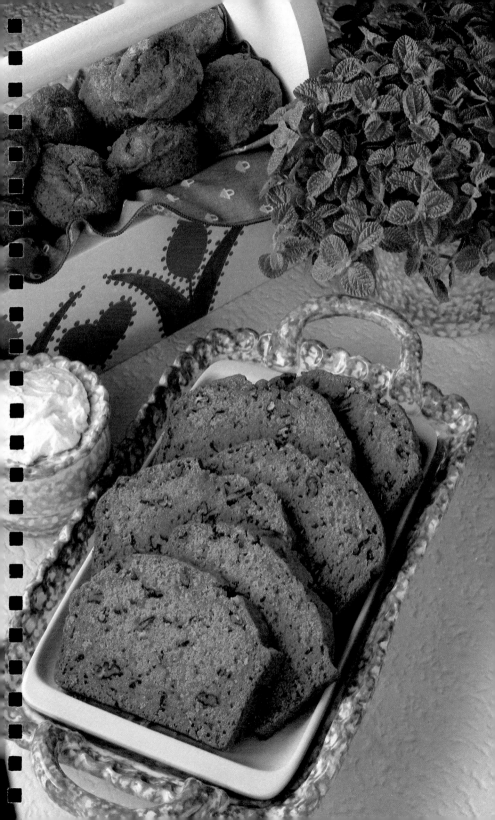

Cinnamon Swirl Yeast Bread

Delicious, down-home loaf, golden with pumpkin, swirled enticingly with cinnamon and raisins—destined to become everyone's favorite.

1 package (¼ oz.) active dry yeast
1½ cups warm water (105°F to 115°F)
Sugar, divided
Butter or margarine, divided, melted
2 eggs
1½ teaspoons salt
2 teaspoons ground cinnamon, divided
1 cup LIBBY'S Solid Pack Pumpkin
7 to 7½ cups flour
1 cup raisins, divided

Dissolve yeast in warm water. Add ⅔ cup sugar, ⅔ cup melted butter, eggs, salt and 1 teaspoon cinnamon; mix well. Stir in pumpkin and 3 cups flour; beat until smooth. Add enough remaining flour to form soft dough. On floured surface, knead dough until smooth and elastic. Place in greased bowl; brush with melted butter. Cover; let rise in warm place until double in volume, about 1½ hours. Punch down dough; divide in half. On lightly floured surface, roll out each half into one 18x9-inch rectangle. Brush each rectangle with 2 tablespoons melted butter; sprinkle with half of combined ½ cup sugar and 1 teaspoon cinnamon. Sprinkle each with ½ cup of raisins. Roll up from narrow end; press ends to seal. Fold ends under loaves; place each, seam side down, in greased, 9x5-inch loaf pan. Cover; let rise until double in volume, about 1 hour. Preheat oven to 375°F. Brush loaves lightly with additional melted butter. Bake 50 to 55 minutes or until golden brown and loaves sound hollow when tapped. Remove from pans; cool on wire rack. Yields 2 loaves.

VARIATION:

For a sweeter bread, combine 1 cup powdered sugar and 5 to 6 tablespoons cream or milk to make a glaze consistency. Drizzle over loaves.

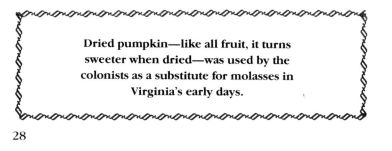

Dried pumpkin—like all fruit, it turns sweeter when dried—was used by the colonists as a substitute for molasses in Virginia's early days.

Spiced Bubble Bread

A serve-with-pride spectacular: break-apart yeast bread, rich with pumpkin and nuts and spices, baked to a golden brown in an angel-cake pan

2 teaspoons ground cinnamon
½ teaspoon ground cloves
½ teaspoon ground ginger
½ teaspoon ground nutmeg
1 package (¼ oz.) active dry yeast
1 cup warm water (105°F to 115°F)

1½ cups sugar, divided
14 tablespoons butter, divided, melted
1 teaspoon salt
½ cup nonfat dry milk solids
1 can (16 oz.) LIBBY'S Solid Pack Pumpkin
5 cups flour
½ cup finely chopped nuts

Combine spices, mixing well; set aside. In large mixer bowl, dissolve yeast in water. Stir in ½ cup sugar, 6 tablespoons butter, salt, dry milk and pumpkin. Add 2 teaspoons of spice mixture and 2½ cups flour. Beat on low speed 3 minutes, scraping bowl often. Gradually beat in enough remaining flour, about 2½ cups, to form a stiff dough. On lightly floured surface, knead until smooth, adding flour as needed. Place in greased bowl. Cover; let rise in warm place until double in volume, about 1½ hours. Lightly grease a 10-inch tube pan; if pan has removable bottom, line the bottom and sides with foil. Combine remaining spice mixture and 1 cup sugar; mix well. Punch down dough; divide into thirds. Shape each third into a smooth 18-inch rope; cut each into eighteen equal pieces. Shape pieces into smooth balls. Dip each ball in remaining melted butter and roll in sugar mixture. Arrange eighteen balls in a single layer in bottom of pan so they just touch; sprinkle with one-third of the nuts. Top with two remaining layers of eighteen balls each, staggering balls; sprinkle each layer with remaining nuts. Cover pan lightly; let rise in warm place, about 45 minutes. Preheat oven to 325°F. Bake 70 minutes, or until golden brown. Cool on wire rack 20 minutes; invert onto serving plate. To serve, break apart with forks. Yields 12 servings.

The West Indian pumpkin, known as calabaza, is a culinary favorite in the Caribbean and throughout Latin America.

Pumpkin-Eater Doughnuts

Here's a surprise—good-for-you doughnuts! Delicious, too, they are made with bran cereal and flavored with pumpkin pie spice.

2 tablespoons shortening	2¾ cups flour
¾ cup sugar	2 teaspoons baking powder
2 eggs	1 teaspoon pumpkin pie
1 cup LIBBY'S Solid Pack	spice
Pumpkin	½ teaspoon salt
1 cup shredded bran cereal	Oil

In large bowl, cream shortening and sugar until light and fluffy. Add eggs, one at a time, mixing well after each addition. Add pumpkin and cereal; mix well. Let stand 2 minutes. Sift flour, baking powder, spice and salt together; stir into pumpkin mixture, half at a time. Cover; chill 1 hour or until dough is stiff enough to handle. On lightly floured surface, roll out to ½-inch thickness. Cut with 2½-inch doughnut cutter. In large pan, heat 2 inches of oil to 375°F. Fry doughnuts, a few at a time, until golden brown and thoroughly cooked, about 1 minute on each side. Drain on paper towel on wire rack. Repeat with trimmings to use all dough. Dip cooled doughnuts into cinnamon sugar or powdered sugar, if desired. Yields 1½ dozen.

Honey-Wheat Pumpkin Muffins

The goodness is whole wheat flour and pumpkin, the sweetness is honey—these special muffins start the day right.

1 cup LIBBY'S Solid Pack	1 cup whole wheat flour
Pumpkin	1 cup all-purpose flour
1 cup milk	½ cup sugar
¼ cup butter or margarine,	1 tablespoon baking powder
melted	¼ teaspoon salt
¼ cup honey	½ cup chopped walnuts
1 egg, slightly beaten	

Preheat oven to 400°F. Combine pumpkin, milk, butter, honey and egg; mix well. Combine flours, sugar, baking powder, salt and nuts. Add to pumpkin mixture, mixing until just moistened. Spoon into greased medium-size muffin pans, filling each cup half full. Bake 15 minutes. Yields 1½ dozen.

Spiced Bubble Bread, Cinnamon Swirl Yeast Bread,
Pumpkin-Go-Round Coffee Cake

31

Streusel Swirl Coffee Cake

Tastily marbled with pumpkin pie mix, this great brunch-time favorite is topped with a crumbly brown sugar-cinnamon mixture and served warm.

Butter or margarine, softened
1 cup granulated sugar
2 eggs
1 teaspoon vanilla extract
2½ cups flour, divided
1 tablespoon baking powder
½ teaspoon salt

1 cup milk
½ cup LIBBY'S Pumpkin Pie Mix
¾ teaspoon ground cinnamon, divided
⅔ cup firmly packed brown sugar

Preheat oven to 350°F. Cream ⅓ cup butter and granulated sugar until light and fluffy. Blend in eggs and vanilla. Combine 2 cups flour, baking powder and salt; add alternately with milk, mixing well after each addition. Reserve 1 cup batter. Pour remaining batter into greased and floured 13x9-inch baking pan. Combine reserved batter with pumpkin pie mix and ¼ teaspoon cinnamon. Drop pumpkin mixture over plain batter, swirl with knife for marble effect. Bake 20 minutes. Combine brown sugar, ½ cup flour and ½ teaspoon cinnamon; cut in ¼ cup butter until mixture resembles coarse crumbs. Sprinkle over cake; continue baking 10 minutes. Serve warm. Yields 10 to 12 servings.

The bigger the pumpkin, the better its eating quality? Actually, the reverse is more likely to be true. Pumpkins for peak-quality canned pumpkin are generally harvested when they're 10 to 15 pounds in weight—because the flesh of larger-sized pumpkins is invariably coarser.

Indian Corn Bread

*This improvement on an old standby produces a moist,
flavorful, pumpkin-golden bread that's delicious served with
butter and/or honey.*

1 cup flour
1 cup cornmeal
⅓ cup sugar
2 teaspoons baking powder
½ teaspoon salt

1 cup LIBBY'S Solid Pack
   Pumpkin
¼ cup butter or margarine,
   melted
2 eggs

Preheat oven to 425°F. In medium bowl, combine flour, cornmeal, sugar, baking powder and salt; mix well. Add combined
remaining ingredients; beat vigorously 1 minute. Spread batter
evenly into greased 8x8-inch baking pan. Bake 20 to 25 minutes
or until golden brown. Cut into squares. Serve with butter and/
or honey, if desired. Yields 6 servings.

Pumpkin Pancakes

*Weekend breakfast treat for the whole family—these lightly
spiced griddle cakes are golden with pumpkin's natural color
and delicate flavor.*

2 cups flour
2 tablespoons firmly packed
   brown sugar
1 tablespoon baking powder
1 teaspoon salt
1 teaspoon ground cinnamon
¼ teaspoon ground nutmeg

¼ teaspoon ground ginger
1½ cups milk
½ cup LIBBY'S Solid Pack
   Pumpkin
1 egg, slightly beaten
2 tablespoons oil

Preheat lightly oiled griddle to 375°F. In large bowl, combine dry
ingredients. In separate bowl, combine remaining ingredients;
mix well. Add to flour mixture, stirring until just moistened
(batter will be very thick). For each pancake, pour ¼ cup batter
onto hot griddle. Using a spatula, spread batter into a 4-inch
circle before mixture sets. Cook until surface bubbles and ap-
pears dry. Turn; continue cooking 2 to 3 minutes. Serve with
butter and maple syrup. Yields about 16 pancakes.

Sunday Special Waffles

Top this pecan-studded waffle favorite with whipped cream for a bountiful breakfast or brunch.

2½ cups sifted cake flour
  4 teaspoons baking powder
  2 teaspoons ground cinnamon
  1 teaspoon salt
 ¼ teaspoon ground nutmeg
  3 eggs, separated

1¾ cups milk
 ½ cup LIBBY'S Solid Pack Pumpkin
 ½ cup butter or margarine, melted
  1 cup chopped pecans

Preheat waffle iron. In large bowl, sift together dry ingredients. In medium bowl, beat egg yolks. Add milk, pumpkin and butter; mix well. Add to dry ingredients, mixing until thoroughly blended. Stir in nuts. Beat egg whites until stiff peaks form. Fold into batter. Pour 1 cup batter onto hot, lightly oiled waffle iron. Cook 3 to 5 minutes or until golden brown. Repeat with remaining batter. Yields 5 cups batter or twenty 4-inch waffles.

VARIATION:
Substitute buttermilk for milk and reduce baking powder to 2 teaspoons.

Apple Pumpkin Fritters

Tart apple chunks cloaked in spicy pumpkin batter—serve them warm, drifted with powdered sugar at breakfast, tea time or supper.

   Oil
 ½ cup LIBBY'S Solid Pack Pumpkin
 ¼ cup sugar
  2 eggs, slightly beaten
1½ teaspoons ground cinnamon

½ teaspoon ground nutmeg
 2 cups biscuit mix
 1 cup chopped tart apple
   Powdered sugar

In 2-quart saucepan, heat 3 to 4 inches oil to 375°F. In large mixing bowl, combine pumpkin, sugar, eggs and spices. Stir in biscuit mix and apple. Drop rounded teaspoonfuls into oil, frying three to four at a time. Drain on paper towel. Sprinkle with powdered sugar. Serve warm. Yields about 3½ dozen.

Pumpkin Butter

Spiced pumpkin, slow-cooked and mellowed with brown sugar and honey, spiked with lemon juice for perky flavor— great on toast or muffins.

1 can (16 oz.) LIBBY'S Solid Pack Pumpkin	¼ cup honey
⅔ cup firmly packed brown sugar	1 tablespoon lemon juice
	¼ teaspoon ground cinnamon
	⅛ teaspoon ground cloves

In medium saucepan, combine ingredients; mix well. Bring to boil over medium-high heat, stirring frequently. Reduce heat, simmer 20 minutes or until thickened, stirring occasionally. Pour hot mixture into sterilized canning jars; seal immediately. Yields 2 cups.

NOTE: Unsealed Pumpkin Butter may be stored in an airtight container in refrigerator several weeks or frozen several months.

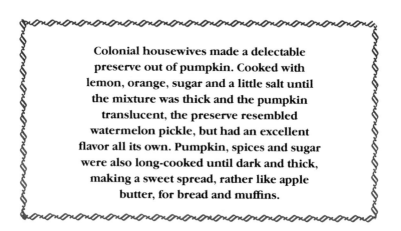

Colonial housewives made a delectable preserve out of pumpkin. Cooked with lemon, orange, sugar and a little salt until the mixture was thick and the pumpkin translucent, the preserve resembled watermelon pickle, but had an excellent flavor all its own. Pumpkin, spices and sugar were also long-cooked until dark and thick, making a sweet spread, rather like apple butter, for bread and muffins.

MAIN DISH/SIDE DISH . . .
FIRST CALL FOR DINNER

Pumpkin points the way to excellent new main dishes, side dishes

Stews and casseroles, pasta and skillet dishes, vegetables and salads—they all roll endlessly through the mind of the home cook who asks the never-ending question, "What shall we have for dinner?" Even more to the point, when the home cook gets stuck in the kitchen rut, as even the best cooks often do, the question becomes, "What can we have for dinner that's new and different?" When that is your problem, it's time for you to start thinking pumpkin. For the heart of the meal, for main dishes and side dishes? Yes, indeed! Pumpkin offers such a deliciously familiar flavor and texture that you will never have to "sell" it to your family. When you want a new and welcome change for main dishes and side dishes, bring out a can of pumpkin and get cooking!

Country Salad with Pompion Dressing

In olden times, the French called pumpkin "pompion," and you'll call this excellent French-type dressing the perfect finishing touch for green salad.

POMPION DRESSING:

¾ cup LIBBY'S Solid Pack Pumpkin
½ cup oil
⅓ cup lemon juice
¼ cup honey
3 tablespoons cider vinegar
1 tablespoon paprika
2 teaspoons Worcestershire sauce

2 teaspoons grated onion
2 teaspoons prepared mustard
1½ teaspoons salt
½ teaspoon celery seed
Dash garlic powder

Combine ingredients in blender container. Cover; blend at medium-high speed 3 minutes or until well-blended. Cover; refrigerate until ready to use. Yields 2 cups.

SALAD:

½ head iceberg lettuce
½ cup chopped green pepper
½ cup radish slices
⅓ cup chopped carrot
⅓ cup chopped onion

1 large tomato, chopped
2 stalks celery, chopped
4 slices bacon, crisply cooked, crumbled

In large bowl, tear lettuce into bite-size pieces. Add remaining ingredients. Toss with ½ cup Pompion Dressing. Serve immediately. Yields 4 to 6 servings.

> In 1671, a cookbook published in New England referred to "pompion sause" as an "ancient New England standing-dish," and bonneted housewives were trading recipes for "pompion pye."

Sunshine Chicken Salad

Pumpkin adds golden goodness to this chicken-with-dill salad mixture to serve in tomato shells, avocado halves, pineapple boats or pita.

¾ cup LIBBY'S Solid Pack Pumpkin
½ cup mayonnaise
1 teaspoon lemon juice
1 teaspoon salt
¼ to ½ teaspoon dill weed
¼ teaspoon pepper

⅛ teaspoon garlic powder
3 cups chopped cooked chicken
1 cup chopped celery
½ cup chopped walnuts, toasted
¼ cup green onion slices

Combine pumpkin, mayonnaise, lemon juice, salt, dill weed, pepper and garlic powder; mix well. Add remaining ingredients; mix lightly. Chill. Serve in tomato shells, avocado halves, pineapple boats or split pita bread rounds, if desired. Yields 4 to 6 servings.

Snow-Top Pumpkin Salad

A glorious medley of pumpkin, yogurt, grated carrot and green pepper in orange gelatin, topped with tangy sour cream.

2 packages (3 oz. each) orange flavored gelatin
1 cup boiling water
1 cup LIBBY'S Solid Pack Pumpkin
1 cup plain yogurt
½ cup mayonnaise
½ cup evaporated milk

1½ cups grated carrot
2 tablespoons grated geeen pepper
1 tablespoon grated onion
1 tablespoon prepared horseradish
Dairy sour cream
Lettuce leaves

Dissolve gelatin in boiling water; cool. In large bowl, combine pumpkin, yogurt, mayonnaise and milk; mix well. Gradually add gelatin to pumpkin mixture. Chill until partially set. Fold in carrot, green pepper, onion and horseradish. Pour into lightly oiled 8-inch square pan; chill until firm. Top with thin layer of sour cream; cut into squares. Serve on lettuce. Garnish with green pepper strips, if desired. Yields 9 servings.

> **Caribbean and Far Eastern cuisines traditionally offer curried pumpkin dishes.**

Savory Pumpkin Quiche

Pumpkin blends perfectly with bacon, onion, mushrooms and green pepper in a savory dish for a brunch or light supper.

1 can (16 oz.) LIBBY'S Solid Pack Pumpkin
½ pound bacon, crisply cooked, crumbled
¼ cup finely chopped onion
¼ cup chopped green pepper
1 jar (2½ oz.) sliced mushrooms, drained
2 eggs, slightly beaten
1 can (12-13 oz.) evaporated milk
½ cup grated parmesan cheese
2 tablespoons flour
1 10-inch unbaked pie shell

Preheat oven to 375°F. Combine pumpkin, bacon, onion, green pepper, mushrooms and eggs; mix well. Gradually add milk, stirring until blended. Toss cheese with flour. Fold into pumpkin mixture. Pour into pie shell. Bake 60 minutes or until knife inserted near center comes out clean. Yields 8 to 10 servings.

Reuben Noodle Casserole

Enjoy Reuben sandwiches? You'll enjoy these pumpkin-sauced noodles, combined with corned beef, cheese and sauerkraut, even more!

1 can (16 oz.) LIBBY'S Solid Pack Pumpkin
2 cups (8 oz.) shredded Swiss cheese
8 ounces noodles, cooked, drained
1 cup crumbled canned corned beef
¾ cup well-drained sauerkraut
5 eggs, beaten
½ cup Thousand Island dressing
½ teaspoon caraway seeds

Preheat oven to 350°F. Combine all ingredients; mix well. Spoon into greased 11¾x7½-inch baking dish. Cover; bake 30 minutes. Uncover; continue baking 15 minutes. Let stand 10 minutes; cut into squares. Serve with additional Thousand Island dressing, if desired. Yields 8 servings.

MICROWAVE:

Prepare as directed. Spoon into greased 11¾x7½-inch baking dish. Cook on High (100%) 15 to 20 minutes or until thoroughly heated. Let stand 10 minutes; cut into squares.

Szechwan-Style Chicken

Traditionally, Szechwan food is hot and spicy—give this chicken right-for-you flavor by adjusting the amount of red pepper flakes.

1 can (16 oz.) LIBBY'S Solid Pack Pumpkin
½ cup firmly packed brown sugar
¼ cup soy sauce
2 tablespoons cider vinegar
2 teaspoons minced garlic
½ to 1 teaspoon crushed red pepper flakes
1 cup water

2 tablespoons oil
½ cup finely chopped green pepper
3 to 3½ pound broiler-fryer chicken, cut up
½ cup chopped dry roasted peanuts
Hot cooked rice

In large bowl, combine pumpkin, sugar, soy sauce, vinegar, garlic and red pepper; mix well. Stir in water. Heat oil in large skillet, Dutch oven or electric fry pan. Add green pepper; sauté 1 minute. Remove peppers with slotted spoon; add to pumpkin mixture. Brown chicken in oil that remains in skillet, using additional oil if needed; drain. Sprinkle nuts over chicken. Pour pumpkin mixture over chicken. Cover; simmer 30 to 40 minutes or until chicken is tender, basting occasionally with sauce. Add a little water to thin sauce, if needed. Spoon hot rice onto large platter. Arrange chicken pieces over rice. Spoon about 1 cup sauce over chicken. Serve with remaining sauce. Yields 6 to 8 main dish servings.

> **In North Africa, pumpkin is a common component of stews. Meat is simmered with onions, pumpkin, and usually some kind of beans, and seasoned with a pod or two of pepper. Rice is the accompaniment.**

Szechwan-Style Chicken, Crepes Florentine, Piñata Pumpkin Chili

Pumpkin Pasta with Walnut Cream Sauce

Golden pumpkin noodles (made by hand or with a pasta machine), served with grated cheese and butter or a creamy walnut sauce.

¾ cup LIBBY'S Solid Pack Pumpkin
2 egg yolks, slightly beaten
1 pound (about 3¾ cups) flour

1 teaspoon salt
½ teaspoon ground nutmeg

In small bowl, combine pumpkin and egg yolks; mix well. Set aside. Add flour, salt and nutmeg to pasta machine. Turn on machine and gradually add pumpkin mixture. Allow dough to be worked 5 to 7 minutes. Correct dough consistency, if necessary, by adding 1 teaspoon water at a time if dough is too dry, or 1 tablespoon flour if dough is too moist. Pasta will have a dry, crumbly appearance, but should feel moist to the touch. Extrude pasta, using disk shape of your choice. Cut to desired length. Pasta may be cooked immediately or dried on a rack or lightly floured surface. Serve with butter, grated parmesan cheese or Walnut Cream Sauce. Yields about 1 pound uncooked pasta.

VARIATION:

For handmade pasta, combine 2 cups flour, 1 teaspoon salt and ½ teaspoon ground nutmeg; mix well. On a clean smooth surface, mound dry ingredients; make a well in the center. In small bowl, combine ¾ cup pumpkin and 2 whole eggs; mix well. Pour into center of mound. Gradually work flour into egg mixture, incorporating as much flour as possible to form a stiff ball. Clean work surface. On lightly floured surface, knead dough 8 to 10 minutes or until dough is smooth and elastic. Cover; let stand 5 minutes. On lightly floured surface, roll out dough to an even ⅛-inch thickness, using a long tapered rolling pin. Loosely roll dough from narrow end. Using a sharp knife, cut roll into slices of desired width: ¼-inch for fettuccine, ⅛-inch for linguine. Gently shake slices to unroll and separate. Cook in boiling salted water 1½ to 2 minutes or dry on lightly floured surface. Cook dried pasta 5 to 6 minutes.

WALNUT CREAM SAUCE:

1 small clove garlic, peeled
½ teaspoon salt
1 cup whipping cream, divided
1 teaspoon dried marjoram
¼ cup olive oil

1 cup chopped walnuts, toasted
½ cup finely grated parmesan cheese
¼ cup chopped fresh parsley
Pepper

In food processor or blender container, combine garlic and salt. Add ½ cup cream and marjoram. Cover; process or blend on medium speed 30 seconds while gradually adding oil. Add remaining cream. Process 20 seconds or until mixture is fluffy. Stir in nuts, cheese and parsley. Toss immediately with hot pasta, mixing until noodles are well-coated. Sprinkle with additional chopped parsley, if desired. Grind fresh black pepper over each serving. Yields sauce for 1 pound pasta.

Golden Harvest Stuffing

This dressing, crunchy with pecans, is outstanding as a casserole or poultry stuffing.

1 cup chopped celery
¾ cup chopped onion
3 tablespoons butter or margarine
1 can (10¾ oz.) chicken broth
1 cup LIBBY'S Solid Pack Pumpkin

1 cup chopped pecans
1 cup orange sections
½ teaspoon salt
¼ teaspoon pepper
5 cups plain croutons

Preheat oven to 375°F. Sauté celery and onion in butter. Add broth, pumpkin, nuts, oranges, salt and pepper; mix well. Toss pumpkin mixture with croutons. Spoon into 2-quart casserole. Bake 25 to 30 minutes or until thoroughly heated. Garnish with celery leaves, if desired. Yields 6 to 8 servings.

MICROWAVE:

In 2-quart casserole, combine celery, onion and butter. Cover; cook on High (100%) 6 to 8 minutes or until celery is tender and onion is translucent. Add combined remaining ingredients; mix well. Cover; cook on High (100%) 10 to 15 minutes or until thoroughly heated, turning dish every 5 minutes.

Betty's Crepes Florentine

Spinach in a pumpkin-cream sauce with Swiss cheese is served with airy pumpkin crepes—a handsome, creative dish for brunch or supper.

1¼ cups flour, divided
½ teaspoon salt
1¾ cups milk
3 eggs, slightly beaten
¼ cup butter or margarine
1 teaspoon salt
⅛ teaspoon pepper
⅛ teaspoon ground nutmeg
2 cups half and half

1 cup (4 oz.) shredded Swiss cheese
1 package (10 oz.) frozen chopped spinach, cooked, well-drained
1 cup LIBBY'S Solid Pack Pumpkin
½ cup slivered almonds, toasted

Combine 1 cup flour, salt, milk and eggs; beat until smooth. Let stand 30 minutes. For each crepe, pour scant ¼ cup batter into hot, lightly greased 8-inch skillet. Cook on one side only until underside is lightly browned. Preheat oven to 350°F. In saucepan, melt butter over low heat. Blend in ¼ cup flour, salt, pepper and nutmeg. Gradually add half and half; cook, stirring constantly, until thickened. Add cheese; stir until melted. Add remaining ingredients. Fill each crepe with ¼ cup spinach mixture; roll up. Place seam side down in 13x9-inch baking dish. Bake 20 minutes. Top each serving with remaining warm spinach mixture. Yields 6 main dish servings.

Pumpkin Barbecue Sauce

Pumpkin and tomato sauce, laced with brown sugar, mustard, onion, garlic and spices—rich barbecue flavor for pork, chicken or beef.

1 can (8 oz.) tomato sauce
¾ cup LIBBY'S Solid Pack Pumpkin
¼ cup cider vinegar
¼ cup firmly packed brown sugar
½ cup chopped onion

2 tablespoons prepared mustard
2 tablespoons oil
1 tablespoon chili powder
1 large clove garlic, minced
½ teaspoon salt

In medium saucepan, combine ingredients. Heat to boiling; simmer 5 minutes, stirring occasionally. Baste on chicken, pork or meat of your choice during last 20 minutes of cooking time. Yields 2 cups.

Golden Harvest Stuffing, Au Gratin Pumpkin Bake

Au Gratin Pumpkin Bake

Thinly sliced potatoes in a rich cream cheese-pumpkin sauce make a delightful side dish.

1½ cups milk
1 cup LIBBY'S Solid Pack Pumpkin
4 ounces cream cheese, softened
¼ cup grated parmesan cheese
¾ teaspoon salt
¼ teaspoon pepper
4 Idaho potatoes, peeled, thinly sliced
6 slices bacon, crisply cooked, crumbled
½ cup green onion slices

Preheat oven to 425°F. In blender container, combine milk, pumpkin, cream cheese, parmesan cheese, salt and pepper. Blend at medium speed until smooth. Blend at high speed for 2 minutes or until light and fluffy. In a large bowl, combine potato slices, bacon and green onion. Pour pumpkin mixture over potatoes; toss lightly until well-coated. Pour into lightly buttered 11¾x7½-inch baking dish. Cover with foil; bake 55 minutes. Remove foil; continue baking 5 minutes. Let stand 5 minutes before serving. Yields 6 to 8 servings.

Piñata Pumpkin Chili

Chili lovers, attention! Here's a new way with your favorite. Pumpkin, replacing tomatoes, "marries" the hearty flavors— sliced ripe olives add extra appeal.

1 pound lean ground beef
½ cup chopped onion
1 clove garlic, minced
1 can (16 oz.) LIBBY'S Solid Pack Pumpkin
2 cups water
1 can (16 oz.) red kidney beans, drained
½ cup pitted ripe olive slices
1 envelope (1.25 oz.) taco seasoning mix
1½ teaspoons chili powder
1 teaspoon salt
1 cup (4 oz.) shredded cheddar cheese
1 cup crushed corn chips
½ cup dairy sour cream

In 3-quart saucepan or Dutch oven, cook meat, onion and garlic until meat is brown. Drain. Add pumpkin, water, beans, olives, taco seasoning mix, chili powder and salt. Bring to a boil. Cover; simmer 30 minutes. Season with red pepper flakes or hot pepper sauce, if desired. Garnish with cheese, corn chips and sour cream. Yields 6 servings.

Stuffed Green Peppers Ranchero

Pumpkin adds a new flavor and moistness dimension to these zesty, meat-filled peppers—with taco chips and a green salad, a perfect meal!

6 medium green peppers, washed and seeded
1 pound ground beef
½ cup finely chopped onion
½ cup finely chopped celery
2 cloves garlic, minced
1 can (16 oz.) LIBBY'S Solid Pack Pumpkin
1 can (8 oz.) tomato sauce
1 cup water
1 envelope (1.25 oz.) taco seasoning mix
3 tablespoons chopped green chilies
½ teaspoon salt
½ cup rice, uncooked
½ cup dairy sour cream
¼ cup chopped green onion

Slice tops off peppers, remove seeds. Cook in boiling, lightly salted water about 5 minutes. Drain. In large skillet, brown meat. Drain, if necessary. Add onion, celery and garlic. In large bowl, combine pumpkin, tomato sauce, water, taco seasoning, green chilies and salt; stir into meat. Add rice; mix well. Cover; simmer 25 minutes or until rice is almost cooked. Preheat oven to 350°F. Fill green peppers with meat mixture. Place in shallow baking pan; fill with ½-inch boiling water. Bake 30 minutes. Top with sour cream and green onion. Yields 6 servings.

MICROWAVE:

Crumble meat into 2-quart casserole. Cook on High (100%) 4 to 6 minutes or until meat is no longer pink when stirred, stirring after 3 minutes. Drain fat. Add onion, celery, garlic, pumpkin, tomato sauce, water, taco seasoning mix, green chilies, salt and rice; mix well. Cover; cook on High (100%) 10 to 15 minutes or until rice is cooked, stirring after 5 minutes. Fill peppers with meat mixture. Place in 8x8-inch baking dish. Cover; cook on High (100%) 10 to 15 minutes or until pepper is tender and meat mixture is hot, turning dish after 5 minutes. Let stand 5 minutes before serving.

> **Pumpkin's closest vegetable-kingdom relatives are cucumbers, melons and the various squashes—all "fruits of the vine."**

Jeannine's Cheese-Stuffed Shells with Spaghetti Sauce

Seasoned ricotta cheese fills pasta shells that are topped with an unusual spaghetti sauce made with meat and pumpkin.

3 cups (1½ lbs.) ricotta cheese	1 teaspoon salt
2 eggs, slightly beaten	⅛ teaspoon pepper
1½ cups (6 oz.) shredded mozzarella cheese	16 large pasta shells, cooked, drained
¼ cup chopped parsley	4 cups Spaghetti Sauce

Preheat oven to 375°F. In large bowl, cream ricotta cheese; blend in eggs. Add mozzarella cheese, parsley, salt and pepper; mix well. Fill each shell with 2 tablespoons cheese filling. Place in 13x9-inch baking dish. Top shells with hot Spaghetti Sauce. Cover; bake 35 minutes. Uncover; continue baking 5 minutes or until thoroughly heated. Let stand 5 minutes. Sprinkle with grated parmesan cheese, if desired. Yields 8 servings.

SPAGHETTI SAUCE:

2 tablespoons chopped onion	1 cup burgundy wine
2 tablespoons chopped celery	1 cup water
3 tablespoons butter	1 teaspoon salt
¾ pound ground beef	1 teaspoon oregano
1 can (29 oz.) LIBBY'S Solid Pack Pumpkin	½ teaspoon red pepper flakes (optional)
1 can (15 oz.) tomato sauce	

In Dutch oven, sauté onion and celery in butter. Add meat; cook until browned. Add pumpkin, tomato sauce, wine, water and seasonings; mix well. Bring to boil. Reduce heat. Cover; simmer 1 hour, stirring occasionally. Yields 8 cups.

Incas of ancient Peru were mainly vegetarians. Although they enjoyed meat and fowl when available, they lived mostly on maize, potatoes, beans, peanuts, avocados, pumpkins and other squash.

Florentine Pumpkin Bake

Spinach and cheeses make this delectable dish a perfect make-ahead for a company brunch.

½ cup mayonnaise
½ cup flour
1½ cups milk
4 eggs, slightly beaten
1 cup LIBBY'S Solid Pack Pumpkin
1 package (10 oz.) frozen chopped spinach, cooked, well-drained

3 cups seasoned croutons
2 cups (½ lb.) finely chopped baked ham, divided
1½ cups (6 oz.) shredded sharp cheddar cheese, divided
5 Swiss cheese slices

Preheat oven to 350°F. In medium saucepan, combine mayonnaise and flour; mix well. Gradually add combined milk and eggs. Cook over low heat, stirring constantly, until thickened. Stir in pumpkin and spinach. Layer croutons in the bottom of lightly greased 11¾x7½-inch baking dish. Top with half the ham, cheddar cheese and mayonnaise mixture. Top with Swiss cheese slices. Repeat layers, using remaining ham, cheddar cheese and mayonnaise mixture. Bake 45 to 50 minutes or until thoroughly heated. Yields 6 to 8 servings.

NOTE: This recipe can be made ahead of time, covered and refrigerated until baking time.

Cheese and Ham Soufflé

Call everyone to supper quickly for this feather-light main dish—soufflés can't wait, neither can the family!

¼ cup butter or margarine
¼ cup flour
2 teaspoons prepared mustard
1 cup LIBBY'S Solid Pack Pumpkin

6 eggs, separated
1 cup ham cubes
1 cup (4 oz.) shredded cheddar cheese
¼ cup grated parmesan cheese

Preheat oven to 375°F. In medium saucepan, melt butter. Add flour, mustard and pumpkin; mix well. Cook, stirring constantly, until mixture comes to a boil. Stir ¼ cup pumpkin mixture into egg yolks. Add egg mixture back to saucepan; cook over low heat 2 minutes, stirring constantly. Remove from heat; stir in ham and cheeses. Beat egg whites until stiff peaks form. Fold into pumpkin mixture. Pour into 1½-quart buttered soufflé dish. Bake 50 minutes or until golden brown. Yields 6 servings.

51

Surprise Cabbage Rolls

Pumpkin with bacon and onion makes the savory filling for rolled cabbage leaves, great to serve as either a side dish or a main dish.

1 large (2 to 2½ lb.) cabbage	½ cup grated parmesan cheese
1 pound bacon, chopped	
1 cup chopped onion	¼ cup chopped parsley
¼ cup dry bread crumbs	2 eggs
1 can (16 oz.) LIBBY'S Solid Pack Pumpkin	1 teaspoon salt
	¼ teaspoon pepper

Remove core from cabbage; remove ten outer leaves. Boil leaves in small amount water 3 minutes. Drain; cool. Chop remaining cabbage. Cook in boiling water 15 minutes; drain. Preheat oven to 350°F. Cook bacon until crisp. Drain fat, reserving 2 tablespoons. Add onion to reserved fat; cook until tender. Stir in bacon and bread crumbs. Combine chopped cabbage, bacon mixture, pumpkin and remaining ingredients; mix well. Fill each cabbage leaf with about ½ cup pumpkin mixture. Place seam side down in lightly buttered 13x9-inch baking dish. Cover. Bake 30 minutes. Yields 10 servings.

Brunch Huevos and Chips Con Queso

Easy-to-do and downright delicious too—eggs scrambled with cheese and green pepper and pumpkin, served over crisp corn tortilla chips.

2 tablespoons butter or margarine	¾ teaspoon salt
	¼ teaspoon pepper
½ cup chopped green pepper	⅛ teaspoon chili powder
6 eggs, slightly beaten	¼ pound pasteurized process cheese spread, cubed
½ cup LIBBY'S Solid Pack Pumpkin	Tortilla chips
2 tablespoons milk or cream	Picante sauce

In large skillet, sauté green pepper in butter. In medium bowl; combine eggs, pumpkin, milk and seasonings; mix well. Pour into skillet. Cook over medium heat, stirring constantly, until mixture is set. Remove from heat; gently fold in cheese. Serve over tortilla chips. Top with picante sauce. Yields 4 to 6 servings.

CAKES/DESSERTS . . .
MAKE WITH EASE,
SERVE WITH PLEASURE
Fabulous pumpkin cakes, tortes, cheesecake,
mousse—and more

A meal without a happy ending is like a story that comes to an
abrupt halt, leaving the points it raises unresolved. If you took
a poll among your family and friends, which happy endings
would win? A high-rise, made-from-scratch cake, gilded with
swirls of frosting or drifts of powdered sugar, or served plain
with ice cream or fruit as a partner? Or perhaps an old-
fashioned pudding or a newfangled one, or a chilled dessert
made early in the day? We all know that pumpkin makes
wonderful pies, but even dedicated pie lovers don't want their
favorite every day. It's time to branch out, to learn what
wonderful cakes, what fabulous desserts you can make with
natural,solid pack pumpkin to help you.
They're here, in this section—pumpkin
treats for what many think of as
the very best part of the meal.

Orange Frosted Spice Cake

*An old-fashioned, made-from-scratch layer cake tops its fine
pumpkin flavor with a delicate, creamy orange frosting.*

CAKE:

½ cup shortening
1¼ cups sugar
2 eggs
2¼ cups flour
2 teaspoons baking powder
1 teaspoon salt
½ teaspoon baking soda
2 teaspoons ground
   cinnamon
1 teaspoon ground nutmeg
½ teaspoon ground ginger
1 cup LIBBY'S Solid Pack
   Pumpkin
½ cup milk
½ cup finely chopped nuts

Preheat oven to 350°F. In mixing bowl, cream shortening and
sugar until light and fluffy; blend in eggs. Sift flour, baking powder,
salt, baking soda and spices together. Combine pumpkin and
milk. Add dry ingredients and pumpkin mixture alternately to
egg mixture, beginning and ending with dry ingredients. Stir in
chopped nuts; spread batter into two greased and floured 9-inch
layer pans. Bake 30 minutes or until wooden pick inserted near
center comes out clean. Cool 10 minutes, remove from pan. Cool
completely on wire racks before frosting. Fill and frost cake. Garnish with walnut halves or chopped walnuts, if desired. Yields 1
9-inch layer cake.

FROSTING:

6 tablespoons butter or
   margarine, softened
4½ cups sifted powdered sugar
¼ cup orange juice
1 tablespoon lemon juice
1 tablespoon vanilla extract
1 teaspoon grated orange
   peel
Dash salt

Cream butter and sugar together until light and fluffy. Add remaining ingredients; beat until smooth.

> Beautiful gourd and pumpkin-shaped
> pottery vessels found in pre-Inca burial
> grounds further attest to the abundant
> varieties known to the Indians.

Pumpkin Spice Cake With Orange Frosting, Pumpkin-Patch Cake Roll

Pumpkin-Patch Cake Roll

Lightly spiced pumpkin cake is filled with a fluffy cream cheese mixture, frosted with chocolate, decorated with pumpkin candies.

CAKE:

- 3 eggs, separated
- ¾ cup firmly packed brown sugar
- ½ cup LIBBY'S Solid Pack Pumpkin
- ¾ cup flour
- ½ teaspoon baking powder
- ½ teaspoon baking soda
- ½ teaspoon ground cinnamon
- ¼ teaspoon salt
- ¼ teaspoon ground cloves

Preheat oven to 350°F. In small mixing bowl, beat egg yolks until thick, about 5 minutes. Gradually add sugar; beat well. Stir in pumpkin. Sift together dry ingredients; fold into egg mixture. Beat egg whites until stiff peaks form. Fold into batter. Spread evenly into greased and floured waxed paper lined 15½x10½x1-inch jelly roll pan. Bake 14 to 18 minutes. Immediately loosen sides of cake. Invert onto towel lightly dusted with powdered sugar. Remove waxed paper. Starting from narrow end, roll cake in towel. Cool on wire rack. Unroll cake; spread with cream cheese filling.

FILLING AND FROSTING:

- 1 package (8 oz.) cream cheese, softened
- 6 tablespoons butter or margarine, softened
- 1 cup sifted powdered sugar
- 1 teaspoon vanilla extract
- Chocolate frosting

Combine cream cheese and butter. Cream until fluffy. Gradually add sugar and vanilla; beat until well-blended. Spread over cool, unrolled cake. Roll; frost with your favorite chocolate frosting. Decorate cake roll with large or small orange gumdrops, using green frosting for stems, if desired. Yields 10 servings.

> Elegant French restaurants, both here and abroad, feature smooth pumpkin soups and rich pumpkin custard desserts.

Southern Delight Cheesecake, Velvet Mousse

Velvet Mousse

An airy, rum-flavored pumpkin-cream cheese mixture with orange juice and spices, topped with a lattice of whipped cream and crystallized ginger.

1 envelope unflavored gelatin
¾ cup orange juice
2 tablespoons rum
1 package (8 oz.) cream cheese, softened
1 cup sugar, divided

1 cup LIBBY'S Solid Pack Pumpkin
⅛ teaspoon ground cinnamon
Dash ground ginger
2½ cups whipping cream, divided

In saucepan, soften gelatin in orange juice. Stir over low heat until dissolved. Cool. Stir in rum. In large mixing bowl, beat cream cheese and ¾ cup sugar until fluffy. Gradually add cooled gelatin mixture. Stir in pumpkin and spices. Chill until slightly thickened. Beat 2 cups whipping cream with 2 tablespoons sugar until stiff peaks form. Fold into cream cheese mixture. Pour into shallow 1½-quart serving bowl. Chill until firm, several hours or overnight. Beat remaining whipping cream with 2 tablespoons sugar; pipe into a lattice design over chilled mousse. Garnish with slivers of crystallized ginger, if desired. Yields 10 to 12 servings.

Quick and Easy Bread Pudding

Pumpkin pie mix and raisin bread make this good dessert a breeze to put together—and you can bake it in the microwave if you wish.

1½ cups LIBBY'S Pumpkin Pie Mix
½ cup milk

2 eggs
8 raisin bread slices, cubed

Preheat oven to 325°F. Combine pumpkin pie mix, milk and eggs; stir in bread. Spoon into 1-quart casserole. Bake 50 minutes or until knife inserted in pumpkin mixture comes out clean. Yields 6 servings.

MICROWAVE:

Combine ingredients as directed. Allow mixture to stand 15 minutes. Invert a small glass in a 1-quart casserole to form a "ring-dish." Spoon mixture into dish surrounding glass. Cook on Medium (50%) 20 to 25 minutes or until knife inserted in pumpkin mixture comes out clean.

Pumpkin Cups

Baked custards, rich with pumpkin, gently spiced with cinnamon and ginger and cloves. Quick-cook in the microwave if you prefer.

2   eggs, slightly beaten
1   can (16 oz.) LIBBY'S Solid
    Pack Pumpkin
¾   cup sugar
½   teaspoon salt
1   teaspoon ground cinnamon

½   teaspoon ground ginger
¼   teaspoon ground cloves
1   can (12-13 oz.) evaporated
    milk or 1½ cups half and
    half

Preheat oven to 350°F. Mix ingredients in order given; pour into eight 6-ounce greased custard cups. Set in shallow pan; fill pan with hot water. Bake 45 to 50 minutes or until knife inserted in center of the pumpkin custard comes out clean. Chill; top with whipped cream and slivered crystallized ginger, if desired. Yields 8 servings.

MICROWAVE:

Prepare as directed. Pour pumpkin mixture into eight 6-ounce buttered custard cups. Arrange custard cups in ring in oven. Cook on Medium (50%) 22 to 27 minutes or until knife inserted near center comes out clean, rotating and rearranging cups after 10 minutes.

Henry David Thoreau, the "Thinker of Concord," who made us so aware of those who march to a different drummer, once said, "I would rather sit on a pumpkin and have a seat all to myself than be crowded on a velvet cushion."

Southern Delight Cheesecake

Rich with cheese and pumpkin and brown sugar, flavored with maple, topped with sour cream and pecan halves—truly, a perfect dessert!

2½ cups graham cracker crumbs
½ cup ground pecans
½ cup granulated sugar, divided
⅔ cup butter or margarine melted
3 packages (8 oz. each) cream cheese, softened
1½ cups firmly packed brown sugar

1 can (16 oz.) LIBBY'S Solid Pack Pumpkin
½ teaspoon ground cinnamon
Dash salt
3 eggs
1½ teaspoons maple flavoring
1½ teaspoons vanilla extract, divided
1½ cups dairy sour cream

Preheat oven to 350°F. Combine crumbs, nuts, ¼ cup granulated sugar and butter; press into bottom and sides of 9-inch spring-form pan. Bake 5 minutes. Combine cream cheese, brown sugar, pumpkin, cinnamon and salt, mixing at medium speed on electric mixer until well-blended. Add eggs, one at a time, mixing well after each addition. Blend in maple flavoring and 1 teaspoon vanilla; pour over crust. Bake 1 hour and 20 minutes. Combine sour cream, ¼ cup granulated sugar and ½ teaspoon vanilla; carefully spread over cheesecake. Bake 5 minutes. Loosen cake from rim of pan. Cool. Remove rim of pan. Chill several hours or overnight. Garnish with pecan halves, if desired. Yields 10 to 12 servings.

As early as some time between B.C. 7000 and 5000, natives in the hills of Mexico began to domesticate some of the wild plants they most enjoyed, including chili peppers, maize and pumpkins which provided both flesh and seeds to eat.

Orange Almond Flan

Light pumpkin custard with a hint of orange flavored liqueur makes its own caramel sauce when served—a lovely special-occasion dish.

1¼ cups sugar, divided
1 cup LIBBY'S Solid Pack Pumpkin
1 cup milk
1 cup half and half

6 eggs, slightly beaten
2 teaspoons vanilla extract
½ teaspoon salt
⅓ cup orange flavored liqueur
⅓ cup sliced almonds, toasted

Preheat oven to 325°F. In large heavy skillet, stir ¾ cup sugar over medium heat until it melts and forms a light brown syrup. Pour into a heated 10-inch quiche dish (shallow baking dish). Holding dish with pot holders, rotate dish quickly so syrup covers bottom and sides of dish. Set aside. In medium saucepan, combine pumpkin, milk and half and half; mix well. Cook over low heat until bubbles form around edge of pan. In large bowl, combine eggs, ½ cup sugar, vanilla and salt; mix well. Gradually stir in hot milk mixture and liqueur. Pour into prepared baking dish. Set dish into a shallow pan. Place on oven rack. Pour boiling water into larger pan to ½-inch level. Bake 45 to 50 minutes or until knife inserted near center comes out clean. Let custard cool; refrigerate overnight. To serve, run a small spatula around edge of dish. Shake gently to release onto a rimmed serving plate. The caramelized sugar forms a sauce. Garnish with nuts. Yields 8 to 10 servings.

In Central America, gourds and squash—of which pumpkin is one—date back to prehistoric times. Although man's chief food in those days was meat, wild-growing fruit such as pumpkin supplemented the meat.

Cinderella's Pumpkin Nut Torte

*Beautiful as a fairy-tale heroine, this dessert presents three
layers of nougat cake with butterscotch-pumpkin filling.*

CAKE:

- 6 eggs
- ¼ teaspoon cream of tartar
- ¾ cup sugar
- ¾ cup firmly packed brown sugar
- ½ teaspoon almond extract
- ½ teaspoon vanilla extract
- 1½ cups graham cracker crumbs
- 1 cup chopped pecans or almonds

Preheat oven to 350°F. Beat eggs and cream of tartar at high
speed, using electric mixer, until foamy. Gradually add sugars;
beat until thickened. Add almond and vanilla extracts; mix well.
Gently fold in crumbs and nuts. Pour into three greased and
floured 8-inch layer pans which have been lined with waxed
paper. Bake 30 to 35 minutes or until cake tests done. Loosen
cake from sides of pans, cool 5 minutes; invert on wire racks.
Cool completely. Fill and frost top of cake with filling. Garnish
with pecans or almonds, if desired. Place cake in refrigerator at
least one hour before serving. Slice, using a serrated knife. Yields
10-12 servings.

FILLING:

- 1 package (3¾ oz.) instant butterscotch or vanilla flavored pudding
- ¾ cup milk
- 1 cup LIBBY'S Solid Pack Pumpkin
- 1 teaspoon ground cinnamon
- 2 cups whipped topping

Combine pudding and milk; beat until thick. Add pumpkin and
cinnamon; mix well. Fold in whipped topping. Chill filling.

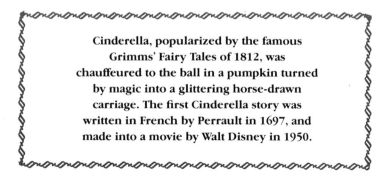

Cinderella, popularized by the famous
Grimms' Fairy Tales of 1812, was
chauffeured to the ball in a pumpkin turned
by magic into a glittering horse-drawn
carriage. The first Cinderella story was
written in French by Perrault in 1697, and
made into a movie by Walt Disney in 1950.

Pumpkin Colada Mousse

Fluffy dessert that tastes like piña colada—serve in individual glasses or, for a special buffet dish, pile into a handsome glass serving bowl.

1 can (20 oz.) crushed pineapple, juice pack
1 envelope unflavored gelatin
½ cup cold water
1 cup LIBBY'S Solid Pack Pumpkin
1 cup dairy sour cream
½ cup firmly packed brown sugar
½ cup shredded coconut
2 tablespoons rum
1 teaspoon grated orange peel
2 cups whipping cream, whipped

Drain pineapple, reserving ½ cup liquid. Soften gelatin in reserved liquid and water. Stir over low heat until dissolved. Stir in pumpkin, sour cream, pineapple, brown sugar, coconut, rum and orange peel; mix well. Chill until thickened but not set; fold in whipped cream. Spoon into 1½-quart glass serving bowl. Refrigerate until firm. Garnish with toasted coconut, orange slices and maraschino cherries, if desired. Yields 8 servings.

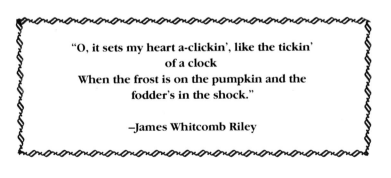

"O, it sets my heart a-clickin', like the tickin'
of a clock
When the frost is on the pumpkin and the
fodder's in the shock."

–James Whitcomb Riley

Dessert Empanadas

Pastry desserts tend to be heavy, but these—tangy with lemon and raisins—are neither heavy nor too sweet, just perfectly satisfying, served warm or cooled.

2½ cups flour
2 tablespoons sugar
1 teaspoon salt
½ cup butter or margarine, melted

½ cup milk
2 eggs, divided
Spicy Pumpkin Filling

Sift together flour, sugar and salt. Add combined butter, milk and one egg; mix well. Form into ball; chill. Divide dough into 12 portions. On lightly floured surface, roll out each portion into a 6-inch circle. Place ¼ cup Spicy Pumpkin Filling on each. Moisten edges with water; fold in half, pressing edges with fork to seal. Brush tops with well-beaten remaining egg. Prick with fork. Place empanadas on baking sheet. Bake at 350°F 15 minutes or until golden brown. Serve warm or cooled. Yields 12 servings.

SPICY PUMPKIN FILLING:

1 can (16 oz.) LIBBY'S Solid Pack Pumpkin
¾ cup firmly packed brown sugar
1 cup chopped pecans

1 cup raisins
1 tablespoon water
1 tablespoon lemon juice
1 teaspoon ground cinnamon
⅛ teaspoon ground cloves

Combine pumpkin and brown sugar. Add remaining ingredients; mix well.

VARIATION:

Prepare and seal as directed. Fry a few at a time in 3 to 4 inches hot oil (375°F) 2 to 3 minutes or until golden brown, turning once. Drain on paper towels. Sprinkle empanadas with powdered sugar, if desired.

> In the celebrated Mother Goose rhyme,
> "Peter Peter, pumpkin eater, had a wife and
> couldn't keep her. Put her in a pumpkin
> shell and there he kept her very well!"

Dessert Empanadas, Almond Bread Pudding, Chilled Pumpkin Soufflé

Almond Bread Pudding

A homey dessert with elegance—made with French bread, pumpkin and spices, almond-liqueur flavored and topped with almond slices.

6 cups French bread cubes
3 eggs, slightly beaten
1 can (14 oz.) sweetened condensed milk
1 cup LIBBY'S Solid Pack Pumpkin
¾ cup firmly packed brown sugar
2 teaspoons ground cinnamon
¼ teaspoon ground nutmeg
2 cups milk
¼ cup almond flavored liqueur
¼ cup butter or margarine, melted
2 teaspoons vanilla extract
¼ cup sliced almonds

Preheat oven to 350°F. Place bread cubes in large mixing bowl. In separate bowl, combine eggs, condensed milk, pumpkin and brown sugar mixed with spices; mix well. Gradually add milk. Blend in liqueur, butter and vanilla, stirring until smooth. Toss lightly with bread cubes. Pour into lightly buttered 11x7-inch baking dish. Sprinkle with almonds. Set dish into a 13x9-inch baking dish. Place on oven rack. Pour hot water into larger dish to 1-inch level. Bake 50 to 60 minutes, or until knife inserted near center comes out clean. Serve warm. Yields 10 servings.

Chilled Pumpkin Soufflé

Pumpkin pie mix and whipped topping make a spectacular dessert the easy way—flavorful, light and lovely to serve in any season.

4 teaspoons unflavored gelatin
¼ cup firmly packed light brown sugar
¾ teaspoon pumpkin pie spice
½ cup milk
1 can (30 oz.) LIBBY'S Pumpkin Pie Mix
2 eggs, separated
2 cups whipped topping
½ teaspoon vanilla extract
½ cup walnuts, coarsely chopped

In heavy saucepan, combine gelatin, sugar and spice. Add milk, pumpkin pie mix and slightly beaten egg yolks. Cook over medium heat 7 minutes, stirring constantly. Chill until cool but not set, about 45 minutes. Wrap a 3-inch heavy duty foil collar around top edge of 1-quart soufflé dish. Join ends with tape. Fold stiffly beaten egg white, whipped topping and vanilla into pumpkin mixture. Spoon into soufflé dish. Chill until firm. Remove collar; press nuts against sides. Garnish with extra whipped topping and maraschino cherries, if desired. Yields 8 servings.

Peanut Brittle 'N Pumpkin Parfaits

Smooth pumpkin pudding alternates with crunchy peanut brittle and fluffy whipped topping in this easy, pretty, so-delicious dessert.

1 package (3⅛ oz.) regular vanilla pudding mix	1 cup LIBBY'S Solid Pack Pumpkin
¼ cup sugar	1 cup whipped cream or topping
¼ teaspoon ground cinnamon	
¼ teaspoon ground ginger	1 cup crushed peanut brittle or chopped nuts
⅛ teaspoon ground cloves	
1½ cups milk	

In saucepan, combine pudding mix, sugar and spices. Add milk; bring to a boil, stirring constantly. Remove from heat; mix in pumpkin. Cover and chill. Spoon into four parfait or any tall, narrow glasses, alternately with whipped cream and peanut brittle. Yields 4 servings.

Pumpkin Charlotte

A happy ending for a summer meal—fluffy filling that combines the flavors of orange and pumpkin, surrounded by delicate ladyfingers.

3 envelopes unflavored gelatin	½ teaspoon rum extract
	Dash salt
1½ cups cold water	2 cups whipping cream, whipped
1 can (16 oz.) LIBBY'S Solid Pack Pumpkin	
	1 package (3 oz.) ladyfingers, split
1 cup sugar	
1 cup orange juice	
2 teaspoons grated orange peel	

Soften gelatin in cold water; stir over low heat until dissolved. In large bowl, combine pumpkin, sugar, orange juice, orange peel, rum extract and salt; mix well. Gradually add gelatin, mixing until well-blended. Chill until thickened but not set. Fold in whipped cream. Line sides of 9-inch springform pan with ladyfingers. Fill pan with pumpkin mixture. Chill until set, 3 to 4 hours. Yields 10 to 12 servings.

Gingerbread Harvest Cake with Yogurt Glaze

The yogurt and wheat germ that add special flavor and texture to this cake will appeal to the health-minded and the dessert-minded alike.

½ cup butter or margarine, softened	3 cups sifted flour
1¾ cups firmly packed brown sugar	2 teaspoons baking soda
	½ teaspoon salt
1 can (16 oz.) LIBBY'S Solid Pack Pumpkin	2 teaspoons ground ginger
	1 teaspoon ground cinnamon
6 eggs, slightly beaten	1 teaspoon ground nutmeg
1 cup wheat germ	½ teaspoon ground cloves
½ cup plain yogurt	Yogurt Glaze

Preheat oven to 350°F. Cream butter and sugar until light and fluffy. Blend in pumpkin, eggs, wheat germ and yogurt. Sift together flour, baking soda, salt and spices. Gradually add to pumpkin mixture, mixing well after each addition. Spoon into greased 12-cup fluted tube pan or angel food cake pan. Bake 50 to 60 minutes or until wooden pick inserted in center comes out clean. Cool 10 minutes; remove from pan. Cool completely on wire rack. Place cake on rimmed plate; spoon hot Yogurt Glaze slowly over cake. Spoon any glaze that drips onto plate back over cake; continue until entire cake is covered with glaze. Yields 10 to 12 servings.

YOGURT GLAZE:

1 cup sugar	1 tablespoon light corn syrup
½ teaspoon baking soda	½ cup butter or margarine
½ cup plain yogurt	1 teaspoon vanilla extract

In saucepan, combine all ingredients except vanilla. Cook, stirring constantly, until mixture begins to boil. Reduce heat; simmer, stirring constantly, for 2 minutes. Remove from heat. Stir in vanilla. Spoon over cake.

VARIATION:

Prepare cake as directed. Spoon into greased 13x9-inch baking pan. Bake at 350°F 55 to 60 minutes or until knife inserted in center comes out clean. Cool; cut into squares. Top with warm Yogurt Glaze.

Cheesy Ribbon Torte

Layers of pumpkin custard and cream cheese filling in a graham cracker crust—make this when you're expecting a crowd of guests.

2 cups graham cracker crumbs
1½ cups sugar, divided
½ cup butter or margarine, melted
2 packages (8 oz. each) cream cheese, softened
5 eggs, divided
½ teaspoon vanilla extract
1 envelope unflavored gelatin
½ cup milk
1 can (16 oz.) LIBBY'S Solid Pack Pumpkin
1 teaspoon ground cinnamon
½ teaspoon salt
1 cup whipped topping

Preheat oven to 350°F. Combine crumbs, ¼ cup sugar and butter; press into bottom of 13x9-inch baking pan. Combine cream cheese and ½ cup sugar, mixing until well-blended. Blend in 2 whole eggs and vanilla. Spoon over crust. Bake 20 minutes. Cool. In heavy saucepan, soften gelatin in milk. Add pumpkin, ½ cup sugar, 3 egg yolks, cinnamon and salt. Cook, stirring constantly, over medium heat 5 minutes or until slightly thickened. Chill until partially set. Beat 3 egg whites until foamy. Gradually add remaining ¼ cup sugar; beat until stiff peaks form. Fold egg whites and whipped topping into pumpkin mixture. Pour over cheese layer. Chill several hours or overnight. Garnish with additional whipped topping, if desired. Yields 12 servings.

> In France, pumpkin is called *"potiron"* or *"courges"* and is used in soups, jams and sweet desserts. It's equally popular across the Mediterranean.

Pumpkin Cake with Coffee Frosting

Two great mixes—pumpkin pie and spice cake—combine with whipped topping to make a moist, fluffy cake finished with coffee frosting.

1 package (18.25 oz.) spice cake mix	4 eggs
1½ cups LIBBY'S Pumpkin Pie Mix	1 envelope (1.25 oz.) whipped topping mix
	Coffee Frosting

Preheat oven to 350°F. In large mixing bowl, combine cake mix, pumpkin pie mix and 2 eggs. Mix at low speed until moistened. Mix at medium speed 2 minutes. Add remaining eggs and topping mix. Mix at low speed until moistened, then at medium speed 3 minutes. Pour into greased and floured 12-cup fluted tube pan. Bake 45 to 55 minutes or until wooden pick inserted in center comes out clean. Cool 15 minutes; remove from pan. Cool completely. Yields one 10-inch cake.

COFFEE FROSTING:

¼ cup butter	1 tablespoon coffee-flavored liqueur
1 cup sifted powdered sugar	Milk

Melt butter in saucepan. Add sugar and liqueur; mix well. Add small amount of milk, if necessary, for drizzling consistency. Drizzle over cooled cake.

Butterscotch Pumpkin Pudding

Two family-favorite flavors, butterscotch and pumpkin, make this easy-do dessert a winner.

1 package (3⅝ oz.) regular butterscotch pudding mix	⅛ teaspoon ground cloves
¼ cup sugar	1½ cups milk
½ teaspoon ground cinnamon	1 cup LIBBY'S Solid Pack Pumpkin
⅛ teaspoon ground ginger	Whipped cream or topping
⅛ teaspoon ground nutmeg	

Combine pudding mix, sugar and spices. Add milk; bring mixture to boil, stirring constantly. Remove from heat; add pumpkin and mix thoroughly. Chill, placing plastic wrap or waxed paper on surface of pudding. Serve pudding topped with whipped cream or topping. Yields 4 servings.

COOKIES/CANDIES/SNACKS . . .
GRAND LITTLE PLEASURES
Great pumpkin cookies, confections and other snack-time treats

We have become a nation of nibblers, a multitude of munchers. Cookies are for eating any time, all the time—even crunchy sweet-with-fruit cookies for breakfast—to the point where an empty cookie jar is a real disaster. The same is true of candies. Those who used to resist "a little something" to take the edge off hunger pangs now snack away happily. We've learned to eat, in moderation, the things we crave, and if we overindulge, we make up for it some other day. And natural, solid pack pumpkin, with its sound nutrition and excellent flavor, can help to produce the very best snack foods while keeping calories under control. Pumpkin is both good and good for you—that's an unbeatable combination.

Pumpkin Pinwheels

These spiral filled cookies, delicious as they are pretty, can be made ahead and frozen—later, slice and bake as the spirit moves you.

FILLING:

1 can (16 oz.) LIBBY'S Solid Pack Pumpkin
1 cup sugar

½ teaspoon pumpkin pie spice
1 cup chopped nuts

In saucepan, combine pumpkin, sugar and spice; mix well. Cook over low heat until thick, about 10 minutes. Add nuts, cool.

COOKIE DOUGH:

1 cup shortening
2 cups sugar
3 eggs, well beaten

4 cups flour
½ teaspoon salt
½ teaspoon baking soda

Cream shortening and sugar until light and fluffy. Add eggs; continue mixing until well-blended. Add flour, salt and baking soda; mix well. If desired, add 8 drops of yellow and 4 drops of red food coloring, mixing until well-blended. Divide dough into three parts. On lightly floured foil, roll each into an 8x12-inch rectangle; spread with one-third filling mixture. Starting from wide end, roll as for jelly roll. Wrap in foil. Repeat with remaining dough and filling. Place in freezer several hours or overnight. To bake, preheat oven to 400°F. Unwrap rolls, cut with a sharp knife into ¼-inch slices. Arrange on greased cookie sheets. Bake 10 to 12 minutes. Yields 7 to 8 dozen cookies.

> In Colonial America, when early crops of barley and hops failed, settlers experimented with local foods. They soon discovered that a very potable brew could be made from fermented pumpkins and persimmons, flavored with maple sugar. It wasn't exactly beer, but it tasted good—and the effect was the same.

Pumpkin Spice Cookies with Lemon Icing, Shortbread Pumpkin Bars, Peanut Butter Jack-O'-Lanterns, Pumpkin Pops, Pumpkin Pinwheels

Oatmeal Spice Drops

For the after-school crowd, glasses of cold milk and a plate of spicy pumpkin-oatmeal cookies add up to a wholesome snack.

1½ cups sifted flour
¾ teaspoon ground cinnamon
¼ teaspoon ground nutmeg
¼ teaspoon ground cloves
¼ teaspoon baking soda
¾ cup shortening
1¼ cups firmly packed brown sugar
1 egg

2 teaspoons vanilla extract
¾ cups LIBBY'S Solid Pack Pumpkin
1¾ cups quick or old fashioned oats, uncooked
¾ cup salted sunflower kernels
½ cup raisins

Preheat oven to 375°F. Sift together flour, spices and baking soda. In large mixing bowl, cream shortening. Gradually add sugar; cream until light and fluffy. Add egg and vanilla; mix well. Add pumpkin and flour mixture alternately; beat until thoroughly blended. Stir in oats, sunflower kernels and raisins. Drop teaspoons of dough on ungreased cookie sheets about 1½-inches apart. Bake 15 minutes or until firm and golden brown. Remove from cookie sheets; cool on wire rack. Yields 4 dozen.

Shortbread Pumpkin Bars

Top buttery shortbread crust with creamy pumpkin custard and, for good measure, sprinkle with streusel crumbs.

¾ cup butter or margarine, softened, divided
⅔ cup granulated sugar, divided
¾ teaspoon vanilla extract, divided
2⅓ cups flour, divided
½ teaspoon baking powder

¼ teaspoon salt
2 eggs, slightly beaten
1 cup firmly packed brown sugar
1 cup LIBBY'S Solid Pack Pumpkin
½ cup chopped pecans

Preheat oven to 400°F. In small bowl, cream ½ cup butter, ⅓ cup granulated sugar and ¼ teaspoon vanilla. Add 1 cup flour; mix well. Press dough into bottom of 13x9-inch baking pan. Bake 5 minutes. Reduce heat to 350°F. Combine ⅓ cup flour, baking powder and salt; mix well. Combine eggs, brown sugar, pumpkin and ½ teaspoon vanilla. Stir in dry ingredients and nuts. Spread over partially baked crust. Combine remaining 1 cup flour and ⅓ cup granulated sugar. Cut in ¼ cup butter until mixture resembles coarse crumbs. Sprinkle over pumpkin layer. Continue baking 25 to 30 minutes. Cool. Cut into bars or squares. Yields 2 dozen 1½-inch squares.

74

Peanut Butter Jack-O'-Lanterns

Peanut butter cookies are good plain, but when you fill them with a spicy pumpkin-raisin mixture, you create something very special.

FILLING:

1 cup LIBBY'S Solid Pack Pumpkin	½ teaspoon pumpkin pie spice
¾ cup sugar	½ cup raisins

In small saucepan, combine pumpkin, sugar, spice and raisins. Cook, over low heat, stirring occasionally, 10 minutes. Chill.

COOKIE DOUGH:

2 cups flour	1 cup smooth peanut butter
1 teaspoon baking powder	2 eggs
¼ teaspoon salt	¼ cup water
1 cup sugar	1 teaspoon vanilla extract

Preheat oven to 350°F. In small bowl, combine flour, baking powder and salt. In large bowl, cream sugar and peanut butter until light and fluffy. Add eggs, water and vanilla; mix well. Add combined dry ingredients; mix until well-blended. On lightly floured surface, roll out half the dough to ⅛-inch thickness. Cut with floured pumpkin-shaped cookie cutter. Place on ungreased cookie sheet. Top each with 1 rounded teaspoon filling. Roll out and cut remaining cookie dough. Top each filled cookie with a second cookie; press lightly at edges to seal. Bake 12 to 14 minutes or until lightly browned. Yields about 18 large cookies.

NOTE: Cookies may be wrapped securely and frozen after baking, if desired.

It is to the early Irish settlers that we owe that most familiar of Halloween icons, the jack-o'-lantern. According to folklore, a stingy drunkard named Jack is said to have been given this feeble light by the Devil himself after being driven from both heaven and hell. With this strange lantern in hand, Jack, in legend, still roams the earth in search of a place of rest.

Pumpkin Spice Cookies with Lemon Icing

Plump with raisins, crispy with nuts, these pumpkin drop cookies owe extra-good flavor to a finishing touch of tart-sweet icing.

½ cup shortening	2½ teaspoons ground cinnamon
1 cup sugar	
2 eggs, slightly beaten	½ teaspoon ground nutmeg
1 cup LIBBY'S Solid Pack Pumpkin	¼ teaspoon ground ginger
	1 cup raisins
2 cups sifted flour	1 cup chopped nuts
2 teaspoons baking powder	Lemon Icing
1 teaspoon salt	

Preheat oven to 350°F. Cream shortening; gradually beat in sugar. Add eggs and pumpkin; mix well. Sift flour, baking powder, salt and spices together; add to pumpkin mixture; mix until blended. Add raisins and nuts. Drop in heaping teaspoons onto greased cookie sheets; bake for 15 mintues or until cookies are firm to the touch. Remove cookies from cookie sheets and cool on rack; frost with Lemon Icing. Cookies may be frozen before frosting. Yields 4 dozen cookies.

LEMON ICING:

2 cups powdered sugar	4 to 5 teaspoons cream or milk
1 tablespoon lemon juice	
1 tablespoon grated lemon peel	

Combine ingredients, mixing well; add just enough cream for spreading consistency.

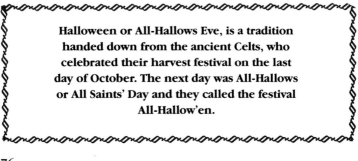

Halloween or All-Hallows Eve, is a tradition handed down from the ancient Celts, who celebrated their harvest festival on the last day of October. The next day was All-Hallows or All Saints' Day and they called the festival All-Hallow'en.

Pumpkin Pops

Nothing could be more fun than a cookie on a stick, unless it's a cookie on a stick frosted with a cheery, grinning jack-o'-lantern face.

½ cup butter or margarine, softened
¾ cup maple syrup
½ cup sugar
1 egg, slightly beaten
1 teaspoon vanilla extract
1 cup LIBBY'S Solid Pack Pumpkin
2½ cups flour
1 teaspoon baking powder
1 teaspoon baking soda
1 teaspoon ground cinnamon
1 teaspoon ground nutmeg
1 cup chopped nuts
Wooden ice cream sticks
Candied green cherries, sliced
Pumpkin Icing
Chocolate Glaze

Preheat oven to 350°F. In large bowl, cream butter, syrup and sugar until light and fluffy. Add egg, vanilla and pumpkin; mix well. Combine flour, baking powder, baking soda and spices; mix well. Add to pumpkin mixture; mix well. Stir in nuts. Drop rounded tablespoons of batter onto greased cookie sheets. Insert sticks into sides of unbaked cookies, insert cherry slice at opposite end of each, for stem. Bake 15 to 20 minutes. Remove from cookie sheets; cool on rack. Frost with Pumpkin Icing and Chocolate Glaze. Yields about 30 cookies.

PUMPKIN ICING:

Combine 1¾ cups powdered sugar with 2 tablespoons water, 2 drops of yellow food coloring and 1 drop of red food coloring; mix until smooth. Frost cookies; allow to dry.

CHOCOLATE GLAZE:

Melt ¼ cup semi-sweet real chocolate morsels with 1 tablespoon butter; mix well. Using small clean paint brush or toothpick dipped in glaze, apply pumpkin features.

> **Old-fashioned Halloween parties were held in the kitchen and all of the rooms were decorated with colorful trophies of the harvest—pumpkins, apples, grain stalks and autumn leaves.**

Pumpkin Buckskin Candy

Chewy, lemon-flavor "leather," made with wholesome pumpkin—kids can roll, stretch and tear it for fun, then eat it as a nutritious snack.

1 cup LIBBY'S Solid Pack
   Pumpkin
½ cup sugar
⅓ cup nonfat dry milk solids

2½ tablespoons lemon juice
1 tablespoon butter or
   margarine, melted

Preheat oven to 200°F. Combine all ingredients; mix well. Line 15½x10½-inch jelly roll pan with foil; secure edges. Grease foil lightly with additional butter. Spread pumpkin mixture evenly in pan. Bake 4½ hours. Remove foil from pan. Starting from wide end, roll foil and mixture; cut into eight slices. Cool. Yields 8 candy-roll servings.

Pumpkin Taffy Apples

Juicy-crisp apples wear a gloriously gooey pumpkin-caramel jacket embellished with crunchy salted peanuts—a spiffy Halloween tradition.

½ cup margarine
¾ cup light corn syrup
2 cups firmly packed brown
   sugar
1 can (14 oz.) sweetened
   condensed milk

1 cup LIBBY'S Solid Pack
   Pumpkin
10 tart medium apples
10 wooden sticks
2 cups chopped salted
   peanuts

Melt margarine in 3-quart saucepan. Stir in corn syrup, sugar and milk. Bring to a rapid boil. Continue stirring over medium heat until mixture reaches soft ball stage (about 237°F). Add pumpkin; return to a boil. Continue cooking, stirring constantly, until mixture returns to soft ball stage, approximately 15 minutes. Thoroughly clean and dry apples. Pierce each apple through core with a stick. Dip in pumpkin mixture; roll in nuts. Refrigerate until serving. Yields 10 servings.

> **Residents of Morton, Illinois, boast of a pumpkin so large it toppled the silo under which it grew.**

*Candied Pumpkin Dandies, Pumpkin Taffy Apples,
Pumpkin Buckskin Candy*

Candied Pumpkin Dandies

Imagine pumpkin, spices and coconut shaped into balls, rolled in chopped nuts, topped with candied cherries. Sound good? They are!

1 cup LIBBY'S Solid Pack Pumpkin
1 cup sugar
1¼ cups flaked coconut, lightly packed

½ teaspoon ground cinnamon
¼ teaspoon ground nutmeg
Finely chopped walnuts or peanuts

In large heavy saucepan, combine pumpkin, sugar, coconut and spices; mix well. Cook over medium-high heat, stirring constantly, about 15 to 20 minutes. Candy is done when it becomes very thick and leaves the side of the pan, forming a ball in center when stirred. Turn mixture onto a buttered baking sheet; cover loosely with foil or plastic wrap. Cool completely. Lightly butter hands and shape candy into balls; roll in chopped nuts. Top each with a walnut or candied cherry half, if desired. Cover and store in refrigerator. Yields about 2½ dozen candies.

VARIATION:

For a crunchier candy, stir 1 cup crushed granola into cooked candy before cooling and shaping.

Frost-on-the-Pumpkin Shake

So easy, so quick, kids can make this blender beverage themselves, combining milk, pumpkin pie mix, ice and orange frost drink mix.

1 cup milk
1 cup LIBBY'S Pumpkin Pie Mix

1 package (2 oz.) dehydrated orange frost drink mix
8 large ice cubes

Pour milk, pumpkin pie mix and drink mix into blender container. Add ice cubes. Cover; blend at high speed 30 seconds or until smooth. Yields 4 servings.

Blonde Brownie Bars

Brown sugar, oats and chopped nuts lend their goodness to these pumpkin treats, melted butterscotch-flavored morsels top them off.

½ cup butter or margarine, softened
2 cups firmly packed brown sugar
1 cup LIBBY'S Solid Pack Pumpkin
2 eggs, slightly beaten
1 teaspoon vanilla extract
1½ cups flour
1½ cups quick or old fashioned oats, uncooked

2 teaspoons pumpkin pie spice
1 teaspoon baking powder
½ teaspoon baking soda
½ teaspoon salt
½ cup chopped walnuts, optional
2 cups butterscotch flavored morsels

Preheat oven to 350°F. In large bowl, cream butter and sugar; add pumpkin, eggs and vanilla. Stir in flour, oats, spice, baking powder, baking soda, salt and walnuts. Spread batter into greased and floured 15½x10½-inch jelly roll pan (or two 8-inch square baking pans). Bake 25 to 30 minutes (30 to 35 minutes for 8-inch pans). Immediately sprinkle butterscotch morsels on brownies; let stand 5 minutes. To frost, gently spread butterscotch morsels. Cool completely before slicing. Yields about 3 dozen brownie bars.

> In Colonial New Haven, blue laws required that all men's haircuts conform to the contours of a cap placed over the head. Since caps were scarce, pumpkin shells were frequently substituted—and the sobriquet "pumpkin head" was born.

Granola Bars

As good as they are good for you, these crispy snacks combine oatmeal, coconut, pumpkin, peanuts and brown sugar for great flavor.

2 cups quick or old fashioned oats, uncooked
1 cup chopped salted peanuts
1 cup firmly packed brown sugar
⅔ cup shredded coconut, toasted

⅓ cup wheat germ
¾ cup LIBBY'S Solid Pack Pumpkin
½ cup butter or margarine, melted
1 egg, slightly beaten

Preheat oven to 350°F. In large bowl, combine oats, nuts, sugar, coconut and wheat germ; mix well. Add pumpkin, butter and egg; mix until dry ingredients are thoroughly moistened. Spread mixture into a lightly greased 15½x10½-inch jelly roll pan. Bake 45 minutes or until golden brown. While warm, cut into 1½x3-inch bars. Yields 30.

NOTE: For crisper bars, remove from pan to wire rack; cool completely before serving.

Pick 'Em-Upkin

Flavorful, quick-energy drink, easy to make in the blender with pumpkin, milk, pineapple juice, honey, wheat germ, banana and ice cubes.

⅓ cup LIBBY'S Solid Pack Pumpkin
⅓ cup milk
⅓ cup unsweetened pineapple juice
1 egg

1 tablespoon honey
1 tablespoon wheat germ
1 small ripe banana
Dash ground cinnamon
2 large ice cubes

Combine ingredients in blender container. Cover; blend at high speed about 2 minutes or until smooth and frothy. Serve immediately. Yields 2 servings.

Pumpkin Date Bars with Lemon Glaze

These easy-to-make bars, prepared with a spice cake mix, will disappear as fast as you bake them.

1 package (18.25 oz.) spice cake mix
1 can (16 oz.) LIBBY'S Solid Pack Pumpkin
3 eggs, slightly beaten
1 cup chopped pitted dates
1 cup chopped nuts
Lemon Glaze

Preheat oven to 350°F. In large bowl, combine cake mix, pumpkin and eggs. Beat until well-blended. Stir in dates and nuts. Spread into greased and floured 15½x10½-inch baking pan. Bake 18 to 20 minutes. Cool. Spread with Lemon Glaze. Cut into bars or diamonds. Yields 2 dozen.

LEMON GLAZE:

2 cups powdered sugar
1 tablespoon lemon juice
1 tablespoon grated lemon peel
4 to 5 teaspoons cream or milk

Combine ingredients, adding just enough cream for spreading consistency; mix well.

Pumpkin Cookie Faces

Kids will want Halloween every day when you make these crisp pumpkin-molasses cookies.

¼ cup shortening
⅔ cup firmly packed brown sugar
½ cup LIBBY'S Solid Pack Pumpkin
¾ cup light molasses
3 cups sifted flour
1 teaspoon baking soda
½ teaspoon salt
½ teaspoon ground ginger
½ teaspoon ground cinnamon
½ teaspoon ground nutmeg
½ teaspoon ground allspice
Icing, raisins, gum drops and other candies

Cream shortening and sugar; stir in pumpkin and molasses. Sift together flour, baking soda, salt and spices. Add to pumpkin mixture, one-third at a time, mixing thoroughly after each addition. Cover; chill 2 to 3 hours. Preheat oven to 375°F. On lightly floured surface, roll out dough to ⅛-inch thickness. Cut with floured pumpkin-shaped cookie cutter (or cut around a floured cardboard pattern). Gently place on greased cookie sheets. Bake 8 to 10 minutes or until firm to the touch. Remove from cookie sheets; cool on wire racks. Decorate with icing, raisins and candies. Yields 2 dozen (3-inch) cookies.

PIES AND TARTS . . .
AS FABULOUS AS THEY ARE FAMOUS
All pies, all pumpkin, and each better than the last

You'll go far and search hard to find anyone to dispute the fact that old-fashioned, custardy pumpkin pie—the kind that Grandma used to make, the kind that always graced the Thanksgiving dinner table—is a first-class dessert favorite. It has been for many generations, it remains so today, and it shows no signs of falling from favor in the future. But even the most devoted buff is generally willing to try something new— as long as it's pie and as long as it's pumpkin, of course! Pumpkin pies by no means begin and end with the old-fashioned kind. That superbly familiar flavor goes on and on — in chiffon pies, in fruited and nutted ones, in tarts, in two- and three-layer pies that rise as high as the pie-eater's eye, in quick/easy chilled pies, and in fabulous make-aheads, all ringing wonderful changes on the family's favorite to make a pie-lover's day.

Pecan Pumpkin Pie

As handsome as it is delicious, this pumpkin-improved version of pecan pie will make the Old South reshuffle its dessert priorities.

3 eggs, slightly beaten	1 tablespoon vanilla extract
1 cup sugar	1 cup pecan halves
½ cup dark corn syrup	1 9-inch unbaked pie shell
1 cup LIBBY'S Solid Pack Pumpkin	

Preheat oven to 375°F. Combine first five ingredients; mix well. Gently stir in pecan halves. Pour into pie shell. Bake 55 to 60 minutes or until knife inserted near center comes out clean. Yields one 9-inch pie.

Northwest Pumpkin Apple Pie

Take a pie poll and you'll find that some opt for apple, some for pumpkin—combine these two and you'll have a real winner!

3 medium apples, pared and cut into thin slices	1 cup LIBBY'S Solid Pack Pumpkin
1 teaspoon lemon juice	1 can (5⅓ oz.) evaporated milk
⅔ cup sugar, divided	
2 teaspoons flour	2 tablespoons butter or margarine, melted
1 9-inch unbaked pie shell with high fluted edge	½ teaspoon ground nutmeg
2 eggs, slightly beaten	1 tablespoon cinnamon sugar

Preheat oven to 400°F. In bowl, toss apples with lemon juice, ½ cup sugar and flour. In pie shell, arrange slices in overlapping circles; cover loosely with foil. Bake 20 minutes. Meanwhile, prepare custard mixture: in medium bowl, combine eggs, pumpkin, remaining ⅓ cup sugar, evaporated milk, butter and nutmeg; mix well. Remove foil from pie shell. Carefully pour custard mixture over apples. Continue baking 10 minutes; sprinkle with cinnamon sugar (a mixture of 1 tablespoon sugar and ⅛ teaspoon ground cinnamon). Continue baking 10 minutes or until custard is almost set. Cool on wire rack at least 2 hours before slicing. Serve warm or cool. Yields one 9-inch pie.

NOTE: Use any favorite baking apple, or, for sweeter flavor, use Red Delicious apples.

Old-Fashioned Pumpkin Pie

Spicier in flavor, richer in color than the famous classic, this is the well-remembered pie that won compliments on Grandma's baking day.

2 eggs, slightly beaten
1 can (16 oz.) LIBBY'S Solid Pack Pumpkin
1 cup firmly packed brown sugar
1½ teaspoons ground cinnamon
½ teaspoon salt
½ teaspoon ground ginger
¼ teaspoon ground cloves
¼ teaspoon ground nutmeg
1 can (12-13 oz.) evaporated milk or 1½ cups half and half
½ teaspoon vanilla extract
1 9-inch unbaked pie shell with high fluted edge

Preheat oven to 425°F. Mix filling ingredients in order given. Pour into pie shell. Bake 15 minutes. Reduce oven temperature to 350°F; continue baking 45 minutes or until knife inserted near center comes out clean. Cool. Yields one 9-inch pie.

California Pumpkin Pie

Three luscious layers: traditional pumpkin pie, then irresistible orange-flavored cream cheese, finally coconut and toasted almonds.

1 can (30 oz.) LIBBY'S Pumpkin Pie Mix
1 can (5⅓ oz.) evaporated milk
2 eggs, slightly beaten
1 10-inch unbaked pie shell
4 ounces cream cheese, softened
3 tablespoons sugar
1 egg yolk
¼ teaspoon grated orange peel
⅓ cup flaked coconut
⅓ cup slivered almonds, toasted

Preheat oven to 425°F. Combine pumpkin pie mix, evaporated milk and eggs; mix well. Pour into pie shell. Bake 15 minutes. Reduce oven temperature to 350°F; continue baking 35 minutes. Meanwhile, combine cream cheese, sugar and egg yolk, mixing until well-blended. Stir in orange peel. Spoon evenly over partially baked pie; sprinkle coconut over top. Continue baking 20 to 25 minutes or until knife inserted near center comes out clean. Cool completely on wire rack. Sprinkle with nuts. Yields one 10-inch pie.

Easy Chiffon Pie

This light, quick dessert for busy days combines a filling made with pumpkin pie mix and a flavorful, no-bake graham cracker pie shell.

1¼ cups graham cracker crumbs
¼ cup granulated sugar
½ teaspoon ground cinnamon
6 tablespoons butter or margarine, melted
1 can (30 oz.) LIBBY'S Pumpkin Pie Mix

1 egg, slightly beaten
4 teaspoons unflavored gelatin
¼ cup firmly packed brown sugar
1 teaspoon vanilla extract
1 cup whipping cream, whipped

Combine crumbs, granulated sugar and cinnamon. Add butter; mix well. Press into bottom and sides of 9-inch pie plate. Chill 20 minutes. In saucepan, combine pumpkin pie mix, egg, gelatin and brown sugar; mix well. Cook over medium heat, stirring constantly, until mixture boils. Remove from heat; chill until partially set. Add vanilla. Fold in whipped cream. Spoon into chilled crust. Chill until firm. Garnish with additional whipped cream, if desired. Yields one 9-inch pie.

New England "No-Crust" Pumpkin Pie

A "miracle" pie that makes its own crust as it bakes comes to the table wearing a looks-pretty, tastes-even-better granola topping.

3 eggs
1 cup milk
1 cup LIBBY'S Solid Pack Pumpkin
⅔ cup firmly packed brown sugar

⅓ cup biscuit mix
3 tablespoons butter
¾ teaspoon ground cinnamon
¾ cup granola cereal with raisins

Preheat oven to 350°F. In blender container, combine all ingredients except granola. Cover; blend at low speed 3 minutes. Pour into well-greased and floured 9-inch pie plate; let stand 5 minutes. Bake 30 minutes. Sprinkle top with granola; continue baking 20 minutes or until center feels firm to the touch. Serve warm or cool. Yields one 9-inch pie.

Posh Pumpkin Pie

Light-as-air pumpkin chiffon mixture, flavored with spices in perfect balance, fills an easy, no-bake graham cracker crust.

1 **envelope unflavored gelatin**	1 **can (16 oz.) LIBBY'S Solid**
1 **cup firmly packed brown**	**Pack Pumpkin**
sugar	½ **teaspoon vanilla extract**
½ **teaspoon salt**	¼ **cup granulated sugar**
½ **teaspoon ground cinnamon**	½ **cup whipping cream,**
⅛ **teaspoon ground ginger**	**whipped**
⅛ **teaspoon ground nutmeg**	**Graham Cracker Crust**
¾ **cup milk**	**Whipped cream and finely**
2 **eggs, separated**	**chopped crystallized ginger**

In heavy saucepan, combine first six ingredients. Stir in milk, slightly beaten egg yolks and pumpkin. Cook over medium heat, stirring constantly, until boiling and slightly thickened, about 5 minutes. Add vanilla. Chill until partially set. Beat egg whites until soft peaks form. Gradually add ¼ cup granulated sugar; beat until stiff peaks form. Fold egg whites and whipped cream into pumpkin mixture. Spoon into chilled Graham Cracker Crust. Refrigerate until firm. Garnish with whipped cream and ginger. Yields one 9-inch pie.

GRAHAM CRACKER CRUST:

Combine 1¼ cups graham cracker crumbs with 2 tablespoons sugar. Add 6 tablespoons melted butter or margarine; mix well. Press firmly into sides and bottom of 9-inch pie plate. Chill 1 hour before filling.

NOTE: Pie can be frozen, if desired.

"And thy life be as sweet and its last sunset sky
Golden-tinted and fair as thy own Pumpkin pie!"

—John Greenleaf Whittier

Posh Pumpkin Pie, Chiffon Pumpkin Tarts

Chiffon Pumpkin Tarts

*Petite tart shells, pumpkin chiffon filling are make-aheads,
so you can easily serve each guest an individual, miniature
pumpkin pie.*

¾ cup firmly packed brown
   sugar
1 envelope unflavored gelatin
1¼ teaspoons ground
   cinnamon
½ teaspoon ground nutmeg
¼ teaspoon ground ginger
   Dash salt

1 can (16 oz.) LIBBY'S Solid
   Pack Pumpkin
½ cup milk
½ teaspoon vanilla extract
1 cup whipping cream,
   whipped
8 baked tart shells, cooled

In saucepan, combine sugar, gelatin, spices and salt; mix well. Stir
in pumpkin and milk. Cook over low heat, stirring constantly,
until boiling and thickened, about 10 minutes. Remove from heat;
stir in vanilla. Chill 1 hour. Fold in whipped cream. Spoon into
tart shells. Chill until firm. Garnish with coconut, toasted pecans
or slivered crystallized ginger, if desired. Yields 8 servings.

Southern Pudding Pie

*Smooth pumpkin pudding, stove-top-cooked, fills this
refrigerated pie; chopped pecans are the finishing touch.*

2 packages (3⅝ oz. each)
   regular butterscotch
   pudding
¾ teaspoon pumpkin pie
   spice
2½ cups milk

1 cup LIBBY'S Solid Pack
   Pumpkin
1 9-inch baked pie shell
1 cup coarsely chopped
   pecans

In medium saucepan, combine pudding and spice. Gradually stir
in milk. Cook over medium heat, stirring constantly, until mixture boils. Cool 5 minutes. Stir in pumpkin. Pour into cooled pie
shell. Cover with plastic wrap or waxed paper. Refrigerate until
firm, about 5 hours. Top with nuts. Yields one 9-inch pie.

> **The first American cookbook, written by
> Amelia Simmons and published in 1796,
> carried a recipe for pumpkin pie.**

Creme Kaffé Pie

The pumpkin-cream cheese filling is coffee flavored; the crust is chocolate crunch—this make-ahead pie is a mocha lover's dream.

CRUST:

1 package (6 oz.) semi-sweet real chocolate morsels	3 tablespoons shortening
	1 cup finely chopped walnuts

In saucepan, melt chocolate and shortening over low heat; stir in nuts. Cool slightly. Spread evenly on bottom and sides of buttered 9-inch pie plate.

FILLING:

1 envelope unflavored gelatin	1 cup LIBBY'S Solid Pack Pumpkin
¼ cup cold water	
1 package (8 oz.) cream cheese, softened	1 cup whipping cream, whipped
¾ cup sugar	
1½ teaspoons instant coffee granules	

Soften gelatin in water; stir over low heat until dissolved. Combine cream cheese, sugar and coffee granules, mixing until well-blended. Add pumpkin; mix well. Gradually add gelatin to cream cheese mixture, mixing until blended. Chill until thickened but not set; fold in whipped cream. Spoon into crust. Chill until firm. Garnish with additional whipped cream and chocolate morsels, if desired. Yields one 9-inch pie.

Chocolate Mousse Pie

Melt-in-your mouth chocolate and pumpkin filling, lightened with whipped cream, in a crunchy, toasted coconut pie shell.

2 cups flaked coconut	¼ pound (16 large) marshmallows
¼ cup butter or margarine, melted	Dash salt
1 cup semi-sweet real chocolate morsels	1½ cups whipping cream, whipped
1 cup LIBBY'S Solid Pack Pumpkin	

Preheat oven to 250°F. Combine coconut and butter; press into 9-inch pie plate. Bake 30 to 35 minutes or until evenly browned. Cool. In medium saucepan, combine chocolate morsels, pumpkin, marshmallows and salt. Cook over low heat, stirring constantly, until morsels and marshmallows melt and mixture is smooth. Cool. Beat with wire whisk; fold in whipped cream. Spoon into crust. Chill. Yields one 9-inch pie.

Luscious Lemon Tart

Light lemon-and-pumpkin custard is a perfect complement for the almond pastry shell and the snowy, high-rise meringue topping.

TART SHELL:

1 cup flour
⅓ cup butter or margarine, softened
3 tablespoons sifted powdered sugar
¼ teaspoon salt

1 egg, slightly beaten
3 tablespoons ground blanched almonds
¼ teaspoon vanilla extract
2 drops almond extract

In medium bowl, combine flour, butter, sugar and salt; knead with fingertips until blended. Add egg, almonds, vanilla and almond extracts; mix well. Shape into ball; knead lightly. Cover tightly; chill 2 hours or overnight. Preheat oven to 425°F. On a lightly floured surface, roll out dough to an 11-inch circle. Press pastry into bottom and sides of a 9-inch tart pan with removable bottom. Trim excess dough. Pierce bottom and sides with a fork. Bake 15 minutes or until lightly browned. Cool.

FILLING AND GARNISH:

5 egg yolks
¾ cup sugar, divided
¼ cup fresh lemon juice
⅔ cup butter or margarine, softened

¾ cup LIBBY'S Solid Pack Pumpkin
1 teaspoon grated lemon peel
⅛ teaspoon vanilla extract
1 egg white

In top of double boiler, whisk egg yolks lightly. Gradually add ½ cup sugar and lemon juice. Cook over simmering water, stirring constantly until thickened, 10 to 20 minutes. Remove from heat; stir in butter one-third at a time. Stir in pumpkin, lemon peel and vanilla. Chill, stirring every 10 minutes until mixture is partially set, 30 to 40 minutes. Preheat oven to 425°F. Pour filling into tart shell.

Meringue: In small bowl, beat egg white at medium speed until soft peaks form. Gradually add ¼ cup sugar, beating until stiff peaks form. Garnish tart with meringue. Bake 5 to 7 minutes or until meringue just begins to brown. Cool on wire rack to room temperature. Chill until serving. Yields 8 servings.

Chocolate Mousse Pie

Microwave Pumpkin Pie

Not one bit of traditional spicy, custardy goodness has been lost in this new-way pumpkin pie—only the appearance is slightly changed.

1 9-inch unbaked homemade pie shell in glass or microwave-safe pie plate	¾ cup sugar
	½ teaspoon salt
	1 teaspoon ground cinnamon
2 eggs, slightly beaten	½ teaspoon ground ginger
1 can (16 oz.) LIBBY'S Solid Pack Pumpkin	¼ teaspoon ground cloves
	1¼ cups evaporated milk

Crimp or flute edge of pastry. Pierce bottom and sides of pastry with fork; place in microwave oven on an inverted 10-ounce custard cup. Cook on High (100%) for 6 minutes, rotating pie plate one-half turn after 3 minutes. Remove from oven; cool.

In 2-quart glass bowl, combine filling ingredients in order given. Cook on Medium (50%) 8 to 9 minutes or until hot, turning bowl and stirring mixture every 2 minutes. Pour into cooled pie shell. Place in microwave oven on inverted 10-ounce custard cup. Cook on Medium for 10 minutes. Rotate plate one-half turn. Cook 5 to 10 minutes more or until knife inserted into filling one inch from rim comes out clean. Remove pie from oven (it will continue to cook on standing). Yields one 9-inch pie.

Calorie-Trimmed Pumpkin Pie

Pumpkin chiffon with a gingersnap border—delicious and saves over 100 calories a serving vs. regular pie.

1 can (30 oz.) LIBBY'S Pumkin Pie Mix	1 teaspoon vanilla extract
	1 cup whipped topping
1 egg, slightly beaten	Vegetable cooking spray
4 teaspoons unflavored gelatin	¼ cup graham cracker crumbs
	6 gingersnap cookies, cut in half (optional)
⅛ teaspoon ground nutmeg	

In medium saucepan, combine pumpkin pie mix, egg, gelatin and nutmeg; mix well. Cook over medium heat, stirring constantly until mixture boils. Chill until partially set, about 1 to 2 hours. Add vanilla. Fold in whipped topping. Spoon into 9-inch pie plate generously coated with vegetable cooking spray and sprinkle evenly with graham cracker crumbs. Chill until firm. Before serving, insert overlapping cookie halves at intervals around edge of pie plate, if desired. Yields one 9-inch pie.

96

ICE CREAM AND SUCH . . .
MARVELOUS MAKE-AHEADS
*Ice creams and other delectable pumpkin
desserts from the freezer*

If you are old enough to remember sunny Saturday afternoons
on the back porch, with Mom preparing the custard base, Dad
chipping ice and measuring salt, the kids turning the crank
and then licking the dasher, you're old enough to be uncom-
fortable discussing age. But they were wonderful times, those
days of making homemade ice cream. Happily, delectable
frozen desserts are still with us. And they are better than ever,
now that we've learned to use pumpkin as an ingredient.
Pumpkin has excellent texture, its color is appealing, its flavor
is well-liked alone or in combination with nuts, fruit, chocolate—and more. Enjoy it in ice creams and the other frozen
delights you'll discover in this selection of sumptuous
desserts.

Pumpkin Sno-Balls

Easy to make and pretty-to-serve, these individual ice cream desserts are even better topped with chocolate syrup to enhance the pumpkin flavor.

1 cup LIBBY'S Solid Pack Pumpkin	½ teaspoon ground cinnamon
1 teaspoon vanilla extract	1 quart vanilla ice cream, softened
½ cup sugar	1 cup chopped salted peanuts

Stir combined pumpkin, vanilla, sugar and cinnamon into ice cream. Refreeze 5 hours or overnight. Scoop or shape into balls; roll in peanuts. Place in freezer until serving time. Serve with chocolate syrup, if desired. Yields 6 servings.

Harvest Baked Alaska

Rich brownie base topped with a spectacular dome-molded pumpkin ice cream, finished with a handsome meringue crown.

1 can (16 oz.) LIBBY'S Solid Pack Pumpkin	4 cups whipping cream, whipped
2 cups maple flavored syrup	1 package brownie mix
1 cup chopped pecans	3 egg whites, room temperature
2 teaspoons ground cinnamon	½ teaspoon cream of tartar
½ teaspoon ground nutmeg	½ cup sugar
½ teaspoon ground ginger	½ teaspoon vanilla extract

In large bowl, combine pumpkin, syrup, pecans and spices. Fold in whipped cream. Spoon into 2 to 3-quart bowl lined with plastic wrap. Wrap securely; freeze 8 to 10 hours or overnight, until center is firm. Prepare brownie mix as directed on package; pour into generously greased and floured 9-inch round baking pan. Bake as package directs. Cool completely on wire rack. Remove from pan; place on oven proof dish. Unmold filling onto brownie. Cover with foil; place in freezer. Fifteen minutes before serving, remove filling and brownie from freezer. Preheat oven to 475°F. In small mixer bowl, beat egg whites until foamy. Add cream of tartar; beat until soft peaks form. Gradually add sugar, beating at high speed until stiff peaks form. Fold in vanilla. Spread meringue over filling and brownie, making sure all edges are sealed. Bake on lower rack in oven 4 minutes or until meringue begins to brown. Serve immediately. Yields 8 to 10 servings.

Harvest Baked Alaska

Pumpkin Swirl Ice Cream 'N Cookie Pie

The surprise here is a wonderfully unusual crust; the bonus is that you can make and freeze this pie ahead, serve to unexpected guests.

COOKIE CRUSTS:

1 cup butter or margarine	2 cups flour
¼ cup sugar	½ cup finely chopped nuts

Preheat oven to 375°F. Cream butter and sugar. Add flour, mixing just until dough will form a ball. Stir in nuts. Press dough evenly over bottom and sides of two 9-inch pie pans, using well-floured fingers. Bake 15 minutes or until lightly brown. Cool; freeze until ready to use.

FILLING:

1½ cups LIBBY's Pumpkin Pie Mix	½ cup whipping cream, whipped
¼ cup firmly packed brown sugar	2 quarts vanilla ice cream, softened
½ teaspoon vanilla extract	

In mixing bowl, combine pumpkin pie mix, brown sugar and vanilla. Fold in whipped cream. Place in freezer until partially frozen. Spread ice cream in a flat baking pan. Spoon partially frozen pumpkin mixture over ice cream and swirl with knife or metal spatula. Spoon into frozen crusts; cover with foil. Freeze until firm. Remove from freezer about 30 to 45 minutes before serving. Dip pan into warm water to loosen crust; cut into wedges. Yields two 9-inch pies.

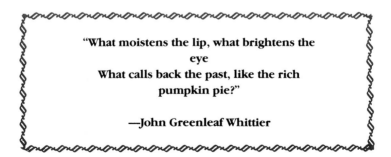

"What moistens the lip, what brightens the eye
What calls back the past, like the rich pumpkin pie?"

—John Greenleaf Whittier

Pumpkin Ripple

You can transform plain vanilla ice cream into something special with pumpkin pie mix, coconut, grated orange peel—and know-how!

1½ cups LIBBY'S Pumpkin Pie Mix
¼ cup firmly packed brown sugar
1 can (3½ oz.) flaked coconut

1 tablespoon grated orange peel
3 pints vanilla ice cream, softened

Combine pumpkin pie mix, sugar, coconut and orange peel. Place softened ice cream into a 9-inch square pan. Stir pumpkin mixture into ice cream, leaving swirls of unblended ice cream. Freeze. Thaw in refrigerator about 20 minutes before serving. Scoop into serving dishes. Garnish with additional coconut, if desired. Yields 2 quarts of ice cream.

Ice Cream Cooler

Sometimes a milk shake is the just-right dessert, particularly when it is made with ice cream, pumpkin, coffee and spices.

½ cup milk
1 cup LIBBY'S Solid Pack Pumpkin
1 pint vanilla ice cream
½ cup firmly packed brown sugar

1 teaspoon instant coffee granules
1 teaspoon ground cinnamon
¼ teaspoon ground ginger
¼ teaspoon ground nutmeg

In blender container, place milk and remaining ingredients. Cover; blend at high speed until smooth. Yields 3 cups.

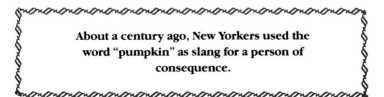

About a century ago, New Yorkers used the word "pumpkin" as slang for a person of consequence.

Orange Almond Sorbet

Orange juice and pumpkin complement one another in this refreshing light dessert; almond-flavored liqueur contributes sensational taste.

4 large oranges, cut in half
1 can (16 oz.) LIBBY'S Solid Pack Pumpkin
½ cup sugar
1 teaspoon lemon juice
Dash salt
1 cup almond flavored liqueur

Squeeze juice from oranges; reserve juice. Remove pulp and fiber from oranges, leaving shells intact. Combine pumpkin, ¾ cup reserved orange juice, sugar, lemon juice and salt; mix well. Freeze in ice cube trays until firm. Dip trays in warm water to release cubes. In blender container, place half of liqueur and half of frozen cubes. Cover; blend at high speed until smooth, using pulse button as needed. Repeat with remaining liqueur and frozen cubes. Fill orange shells with mixture; return to freezer until ready to serve. Garnish each serving with mint leaves, if desired. Yields 8 servings.

VARIATION:

1½ cups fresh or reconstituted frozen orange juice can be substituted for almond flavored liqueur.

Pumpkin Caramel Sauce

Pumpkin is mixed with caramel sauce, lightly flavored with pumpkin pie spice, and served warm to make an elegant topping for ice cream.

1 jar (12.25 oz.) caramel flavored ice cream sauce
½ cup LIBBY'S Solid Pack Pumpkin
½ teaspoon pumpkin pie spice

In medium saucepan, combine ingredients; mix well. Warm over low heat. Spoon over ice cream. Top with chopped nuts, if desired. Yields 1⅓ cups sauce.

VARIATION:

Butterscotch flavored ice cream sauce can be substituted for the caramel flavored sauce.

Pumpkin Caramel Sauce on Ice Cream

Peanut Crunch Pumpkin Pie

Made in no time flat with pumpkin pie mix, this creamy-yet-crunchy peanutty-good pie will rank high on your list of dessert favorites.

2 9-inch frozen pie crusts	1 cup chopped salted peanuts
1 can (30 oz.) LIBBY'S	3 cups whipped topping
Pumpkin Pie Mix	1 teaspoon vanilla extract
¼ cup smooth peanut butter	

Bake crusts according to package directions. Cool. In large bowl, combine pumpkin pie mix, peanut butter and peanuts; mix until peanut butter is thoroughly blended. Fold in whipped topping and vanilla. Pour into pie shells. Freeze until firm, at least 4 hours. Remove pie from freezer 10 to 15 minutes before serving. Garnish with whipped topping and chopped nuts, if desired. Yields two 9-inch pies.

Peace Pipe Pie with Caramelized Almonds

Smooth ice cream and crunchy nuts provide this dessert's splendid contrasty texture; pumpkin contributes uniquely perfect flavor.

1 pint vanilla ice cream, softened	1 teaspoon ground cinnamon
1 10-inch pie shell, baked	½ teaspoon ground ginger
1 can (16 oz.) LIBBY'S Solid Pack Pumpkin	½ teaspoon ground cloves
	1 teaspoon vanilla extract
1¾ cups sugar, divided	1½ cups whipped cream
½ teaspoon salt	1 cup slivered almonds

Spread softened ice cream in cooled pie shell; freeze until firm. Mix pumpkin with 1½ cups sugar, spices and vanilla; fold in 1 cup whipped cream. Pour filling over ice cream. Cover; freeze about 4 hours. Combine nuts and ¼ cup sugar in small skillet. Stir constantly over low heat as sugar begins to turn color. Remove from heat when almonds are caramel colored. Spread on greased cookie sheet. Break apart when crisp. Garnish pie with remaining ½ cup whipped cream and caramelized almonds. Yields one 10-inch pie.

Frozen Pumpkin Bombe

The perfect company-coming dessert can be waiting in your freezer—just let it stand a few minutes, then serve it with well-deserved pride.

2½ cups gingersnap crumbs	½ teaspoon salt
1¼ cups sugar, divided	1 teaspoon ground cinnamon
¼ cup butter or margarine, melted	½ teaspoon ground ginger
	¼ teaspoon ground cloves
2 pints vanilla ice cream, softened	1 cup whipping cream
	1 teaspoon vanilla extract
1 can (16 oz.) LIBBY'S Solid Pack Pumpkin	

Combine crumbs, ¼ cup sugar and butter. Reserving 1 cup crumb mixture, press remaining crumb mixture evenly inside a 2½-quart mixing bowl that has been lined with plastic wrap or aluminum foil. Mold into shape by pressing 1½-quart bowl into center. Remove inner bowl; place crumb-lined bowl in freezer. Freeze until firm. Pack softened ice cream into bottom and up sides of frozen crumbs, using chilled 1½-quart bowl again as mold. Freeze until ice cream hardens. Combine pumpkin, 1 cup sugar, salt and spices. Whip cream until stiff; fold into pumpkin mixture; stir in vanilla. Pour mixture into center of ice cream. Top evenly with remaining 1 cup crumb mixture. Freeze overnight. Unmold by dipping bowl into warm water for a few seconds, lift out with liner and invert on serving plate. Allow to thaw slightly at room temperature 20 to 30 minutes. Garnish with additional whipped cream, maraschino cherries and mint leaves, if desired. Cut into wedges. Yields 12 servings.

> **In China, pumpkins were at one time revered because they were considered to be symbols of success and health**

Frozen Pumpkin Dessert Squares

Wholesome and delicious pumpkin and rich, smooth ice cream combine in a graham cracker shell—a just-right dessert for a summer night.

1 cup graham cracker crumbs	½ teaspoon salt
¼ cup granulated sugar	1 teaspoon ground cinnamon
¼ cup butter or margarine, melted	¼ teaspoon ground ginger
	⅛ teaspoon ground cloves
1 can (16 oz.) LIBBY'S Solid Pack Pumpkin	1 quart vanilla ice cream, softened
½ cup firmly packed brown sugar	

Preheat oven to 325°F. Combine crumbs, granulated sugar and butter; mix well. Press into bottom of 9-inch square pan. Bake 10 minutes; cool. Combine pumpkin, brown sugar, salt and spices. Fold in ice cream. Pour over crust. Cover; freeze until firm. Place in refrigerator 2 to 3 hours before serving. Cut into squares; top each square with whipped cream and toasted coconut, if desired. Yields 9 servings.

Ginger-Snappy Pumpkin Pie

Keep ingredients on hand—the star is pumpkin pie mix—so you can quickly whip up this easy dessert whenever inspiration seizes you.

20 gingersnap cookies (1/3 of a 16 oz. box)	2 cups whipped topping
	¼ cup crushed peanut brittle
1 can (30 oz.) LIBBY'S Pumpkin Pie Mix	

Cover bottom and sides of a greased 9-inch pie pan with whole gingersnap cookies. Place in freezer. In mixing bowl, gently stir pumpkin pie mix into whipped topping until thoroughly combined. Pour over frozen cookie shell. Sprinkle with peanut brittle. Freeze 4 hours or overnight. Remove from freezer 30 to 40 minutes before serving. Garnish with additional whipped topping, if desired. Yields one 9-inch pie.

Frozen Pumpkin Dessert Squares

Midwest Pumpkin Ice Cream Pie

Summer-weather version of baked pumpkin custard pie, this dessert has wonderful down-home flavor that brings folks back for seconds.

1 package (3¾ oz.) instant vanilla pudding mix	1 teaspoon pumpkin pie spice
1 cup LIBBY'S Solid Pack Pumpkin	2 pints vanilla ice cream, softened
¼ cup milk	Graham Cracker Crust

In medium size bowl, combine pudding mix, pumpkin, milk and spice. Mix at low speed on electric mixer, about 1 minute or until well-blended. Gradually add ice cream, about one-fourth at a time, mixing until well-blended. Spoon into crust. Wrap securely; freeze until firm, 8 hours or overnight. Allow pie to stand in refrigerator for several hours before slicing. Garnish with whipped cream or whipped topping and chopped nuts, if desired. Yields one 9-inch pie.

GRAHAM CRACKER CRUST:

1 cup graham cracker crumbs	¼ cup butter or margarine, melted
¼ cup sugar	

Preheat oven to 350°F. In small mixing bowl, combine crumbs, sugar and butter; mix well. Press into bottom and sides of 9-inch pie plate. Bake 8 minutes. Cool.

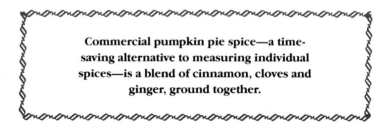

Commercial pumpkin pie spice—a time-saving alternative to measuring individual spices—is a blend of cinnamon, cloves and ginger, ground together.

HOLIDAYS . . . AND
CELEBRATION SPECIALS

*For holiday giving and holiday serving,
dressed-up pumpkin delights*

Special days call for special foods—the fine, best-of-every-
thing treats that bring shouts of joy from children and smiles
of satisfaction to the faces of adults—nostalgic foods that call
up happy memories—innovative ones that promise to found
new traditions. When the home cook begins preparations for
a holiday and looks up treasured recipes, pumpkin will most
likely be on the menu. Pumpkin has a part in so many good
foods, such an abundance of well-remembered delights! And
today, ready-to-use, easy-to-use canned pumpkin will help you
prepare the goodies that play so important a role in the
celebration of holidays throughout the year.

Heritage Pumpkin Pudding with Fluffy Lemon Hard Sauce

Hearty, old-fashioned steamed pudding, rich with raisins, dates and crispy walnuts—serve warm with fluffy lemon sauce.

1 package (18.25 oz.) spice cake mix	1 cup chopped walnuts
1½ cups (½ of 30 oz. can) LIBBY'S Pumpkin Pie Mix	1 cup raisins
	1 cup chopped pitted dates
2 eggs	Fluffy Lemon Hard Sauce

Preheat oven to 350°F. In large mixing bowl, combine cake mix, pumpkin pie mix and eggs. Beat at medium speed 4 minutes. Stir in nuts, raisins and dates. Carefully spoon batter into two greased 6-cup molds; cover tightly with foil and secure with string. Set in larger oven-proof glass bowl. Place on oven rack. Fill bowl with hot water almost to top of mold. Bake 1 hour and 50 minutes or until long wooden pick inserted in center comes out clean. Let pudding stand, uncovered, 15 minutes before removing from mold. Serve hot with Fluffy Lemon Hard Sauce. Yields 10 to 12 servings.

MICROWAVE:

Prepare as directed except increase pie mix to 2 cups. Spoon batter into 3½-quart ring dish. Place dish in oven on inverted 10-ounce custard cup. Cover; microwave on Medium-Low (30%) 40 to 50 minutes or until wooden pick inserted in center comes out clean, turning ¼ turn every 10 minutes.

FLUFFY LEMON HARD SAUCE:

½ cup butter or margarine, softened	2 teaspoons lemon juice
	1 egg, separated
2 cups powdered sugar	1 teaspoon grated lemon peel

Cream butter and sugar; beat in lemon juice, egg yolk and lemon peel. Beat egg white until stiff; fold into sugar mixture. Yields about 1¼ cups.

Carol's Cranberry Nut Bread

For holiday gift-giving, dress up traditional pumpkin nut bread loaves with fresh cranberries for color, grated orange peel for special flavor.

3½ cups flour	¾ cup butter or margarine,
2 teaspoons ground	softened
cinnamon	2 cups sugar
1 teaspoon salt	3 eggs
1 teaspoon baking soda	1 can (16 oz.) LIBBY'S Solid
½ teaspoon baking powder	Pack Pumpkin
2 teaspoons grated orange	1 cup chopped walnuts
peel	1 cup chopped cranberries

Preheat oven to 350°F. Combine dry ingredients; set aside. Cream butter and sugar. Add eggs one at a time, mixing well after each addition. Add pumpkin alternately with dry ingredients. Stir in nuts and cranberries. Pour batter into two lightly greased 8x4-inch loaf pans. Bake 60 to 65 minutes or until wooden pick inserted in center comes out clean. If desired, drizzle with icing (mix just enough cream or milk into powdered sugar for drizzling consistency); garnish with walnut halves and cranberries. Yields 2 loaves.

Holiday Pumpkin Nog

Festive and richly satisfying, this celebration treat combines softened ice cream, milk, pumpkin pie mix and the spirited tang of light rum.

1 quart vanilla ice cream,	1 cup light rum (optional)
softened	Ground nutmeg
1 quart milk	
1 can (30 oz.) LIBBY'S	
Pumpkin Pie Mix	

In large bowl, beat ice cream until smooth; stir in milk, pumpkin pie mix and rum. Cover; chill until ready to serve. Stir just before serving; sprinkle with nutmeg. Yields about twenty 4-ounce servings.

NOTE: For a family party, divide punch in half. Add ½ cup rum to adult portion; leave half plain for the children.

Festive Double Decker Salad

This two-layer gelatin creation offers golden lemon flavor on the bottom, crimson raspberry on the top.

1 package (3 oz.) lemon flavored gelatin
2 cups boiling water, divided
1 cup LIBBY'S Solid Pack Pumpkin
1 cup dairy sour cream
½ teaspoon grated lemon peel

1 cup whipping cream, whipped
1 package (3 oz.) raspberry flavored gelatin
1 can (16 oz.) whole berry cranberry sauce
½ cup chopped walnuts

Dissolve lemon gelatin in 1 cup boiling water. Cool. Stir in pumpkin, sour cream and lemon peel; mix well. Chill until slightly thickened. Fold in whipped cream. Pour into 2½-quart glass serving bowl; chill until almost set. Dissolve raspberry gelatin in 1 cup boiling water. Stir in cranberry sauce. Chill until slightly thickened. Stir in nuts; pour over pumpkin layer. Chill until firm. Garnish with walnut halves, if desired. Yields 6 to 8 servings.

Party Ring Fruitcake

Mincemeat, dried fruit and pumpkin, finished with a drizzle of brandy, make this handsome cake special.

2½ cups flour
½ cup firmly packed brown sugar
1 tablespoon baking soda
1 teaspoon ground cinnamon
½ teaspoon ground nutmeg
1½ cups chopped pecans
1 can (16 oz.) LIBBY'S Solid Pack Pumpkin

2 eggs, slightly beaten
2 tablespoons lemon juice
1½ cups prepared mincemeat
1 package (8 oz.) dried mixed fruit, chopped
¼ cup apricot preserves
¼ cup brandy

Preheat oven to 350°F. In large mixing bowl, thoroughly combine flour, sugar, baking soda and spices. Stir in nuts. Set aside. In another large bowl, combine pumpkin, eggs, lemon juice, mincemeat and dried fruit. Add to dry ingredients; stir until thoroughly combined. Pour into greased 12-cup fluted tube pan. Cover loosely with foil to prevent browning. Bake 60 to 65 minutes or until wooden pick inserted in center comes out clean. Cool on wire rack 10 minutes. Remove from pan; cool completely. In small saucepan, heat preserves and brandy just until preserves melt. Spoon over cake. Garnish with pecan halves, if desired. Cut into thin slices. Yields 24 servings.

Orange-Kissed Mincemeat Squares

Wonderful to have on hand, these squares layer orange-spiked mincemeat, pumpkin-rich custard in a butter crust.

½ cup butter or margarine
⅓ cup sugar
3 eggs, divided
¾ teaspoon salt, divided
¼ teaspoon vanilla extract
1¼ cups flour
1 jar (29 oz.) prepared mincemeat

1 can (16 oz.) LIBBY'S Solid Pack Pumpkin
1 cup firmly packed brown sugar
1 can (5⅓ oz.) evaporated milk
1 teaspoon grated orange peel

Preheat oven to 400°F. Cream butter and sugar. Blend in 1 egg, ¼ teaspoon salt and vanilla. Gradually add flour, mixing well after each addition. Spread dough onto bottom of 13x9-inch baking pan. Bake 10 minutes. Cool. Reduce oven temperature to 350°F. Spread crust with mincemeat. Combine remaining ingredients; mix well. Spoon over mincemeat layer. Bake 60 minutes or until knife inserted near center comes out clean. Cool. Cut into squares; top with whipped cream, if desired. Yields 12 servings.

Pumpkin Country Fruitcakes

No one will know this is an easy, short-cut treat—pumpkin pie mix, date nut bread mix, plus raisins, candied cherries and pineapple.

1 can (30 oz.) LIBBY'S Pumpkin Pie Mix
2 eggs
2 packages (16.1 oz. each) date nut bread mix
2 cups chopped walnuts or pecans

2 cups raisins
2 cups candied cherries, coarsely chopped
1 cup candied pineapple, coarsely chopped
Rum or brandy

Preheat oven to 350°F. In large bowl, combine pumpkin pie mix, eggs and nut bread mixes. Stir in nuts, raisins and candied fruits. Spoon batter into greased muffin pans, filling three-fourths full. Bake 30 to 35 minutes or until wooden pick inserted in center comes out clean. Cool 10 minutes; remove from pans and cool completely. Drizzle with rum or brandy. Garnish, if desired, with additional candied cherries. Yields about 4 dozen.

Spiced Pumpkin Fudge

Fudge made with pumpkin and flavored with spice—a just-right gift-from-your-kitchen for special friends and neighbors.

3 cups sugar
¾ cup butter or margarine
1 can (5⅓ oz.) or ⅔ cup evaporated milk
½ cup LIBBY'S Solid Pack Pumpkin
1 teaspoon pumpkin pie spice
1 package (12 oz.) butterscotch flavored morsels
1 jar (7 oz.) marshmallow creme
1 cup chopped almonds, toasted
1 teaspoon vanilla extract

In heavy saucepan, combine sugar, butter, milk, pumpkin and spice; bring to boil, stirring constantly. Continue boiling over medium heat, stirring constantly until mixture reaches 234°F on candy thermometer, about 10 minutes. Remove from heat; stir in butterscotch morsels. Add marshmallow creme, nuts and vanilla, mixing until well-blended. Quickly pour into greased 13x9-inch baking pan, spreading just until even. Cool at room temperature; cut into squares. Store tightly wrapped in refrigerator. Yields 3 pounds candy.

Pumpkin-Kist Cocoa

Richly spiced hot cocoa, made wonderfully different with pumpkin, is a perfect drink to serve carolers and other holiday-time guests.

1 cup sugar
½ cup unsweetened cocoa
1 cup boiling water
4 cups milk
1 can (16 oz.) LIBBY'S Solid Pack Pumpkin
1 tablespoon vanilla extract
¼ teaspoon almond extract
½ teaspoon ground cinnamon
½ teaspoon ground nutmeg
¼ teaspoon ground allspice
Whipped cream
Milk chocolate morsels or semi-sweet real chocolate morsels

In large saucepan, blend sugar and cocoa. Gradually add water. Boil over medium heat 2 minutes, stirring constantly. Add milk and pumpkin. Heat thoroughly, stirring occasionally. Do not boil. Remove from heat; add extracts and spices. Beat with hand mixer until foamy. Pour into cups. Garnish with whipped cream and chocolate morsels. Yields 8 cups.

Great Pumpkin Cookies

Big, chubby, pumpkin-flavored and pumpkin-shaped—kids love to decorate them, give them to friends as trick-or-treat or party favors.

2 cups flour
1 cup quick or old fashioned oats, uncooked
1 teaspoon baking soda
1 teaspoon ground cinnamon
½ teaspoon salt
1 cup butter or margarine, softened
1 cup firmly packed brown sugar
1 cup granulated sugar
1 egg, slightly beaten
1 teaspoon vanilla extract
1 cup LIBBY'S Solid Pack Pumpkin
1 cup semi-sweet real chocolate morsels
Assorted icings or peanut butter
Assorted candies, raisins or nuts

Preheat oven to 350°F. Combine flour, oats, baking soda, cinnamon and salt; set aside. Cream butter; gradually add sugars, beating until light and fluffy. Add egg and vanilla; mix. Alternate additions of dry ingredients and pumpkin, mixing well after each addition. Stir in morsels. For each cookie, drop ¼ cup dough onto lightly greased cookie sheet; spread into pumpkin shape, using a thin metal spatula. Add a bit more dough to form stem. Bake 20 to 25 minutes, until cookies are firm and lightly browned. Remove from cookie sheets; cool on racks. Decorate, using icing or peanut butter to affix assorted candies, raisins or nuts. Yields 19 to 20 large cookies.

VARIATION: Substitute 1 cup raisins for morsels.

Party Pumpkin Punch

Apricot nectar and tea partner deliciously with pumpkin to make a unique beverage— perfect for any large gathering.

1 can (46 oz.) apricot nectar
1 can (29 oz.) LIBBY'S Solid Pack Pumpkin
1 cup cold tea
1 quart orange sherbet
1 quart cold ginger ale
1 cup vodka (optional)

Combine nectar and pumpkin; mix well. Chill. Just before serving, combine pumpkin mixture and sherbet in punch bowl. Gently stir in ginger ale. Add vodka, if desired. Yields 4 quarts.

Health-Nut Fruitcake

Health-food buffs will appreciate the whole grains, pumpkin and dates in this cake—so will anyone who just appreciates good eating.

1 envelope (¼ oz.) active dry yeast
¼ cup warm water (105° to 115°)
1 cup LIBBY'S Solid Pack Pumpkin
⅓ cup orange juice
1½ cups all-purpose flour
½ cup whole wheat flour
½ cup quick or old fashioned oats, uncooked
1 teaspoon salt
¼ teaspoon ground cardamom
¾ cup chopped pitted dates
¾ cup finely chopped candied cherries
¾ cup coarsely chopped walnuts
1½ teaspoons grated orange peel

In medium bowl, sprinkle yeast over warm water; stir until dissolved. Stir in 1 teaspoon honey; let stand until mixture foams. In small saucepan, combine remaining honey and pumpkin; heat just until warm. Stir pumpkin mixture and orange juice into yeast. Add flours, oats, salt and cardamom; mix until well-blended. Stir in fruits, nuts and orange peel. Spoon into greased 8x4-inch loaf pan. Cover; let stand in warm place 30 minutes. Preheat oven to 300°F. Bake 80 minutes or until wooden pick inserted in center comes out clean. Cool 5 minutes; remove from pan and cool completely on wire rack. Yields 1 loaf.

Long after the Druids, simple-minded country people continued to believe in charms and witchcraft, and especially claimed that on the night of October 31, witches and goblins held revel, and ghosts and fairies danced about in the woods. From these spirits, it was believed, the future could be foretold and human destinies discovered.

Scrumptious Pumpkin Date Torte

Three layers of pumpkin-nut cake—with a richly flavorful date-pecan filling—pretty enough, delicious enough to grace any table on any special day.

CAKE:

½ cup butter or margarine
1 cup firmly packed brown sugar
1 cup granulated sugar
2 eggs, slightly beaten
1 cup LIBBY'S Solid Pack Pumpkin

3 cups sifted cake flour
4 teaspoon baking powder
½ teaspoon salt
¼ teaspoon baking soda
½ cup milk
1 cup finely chopped pecans
1 teaspoon almond extract

Preheat oven to 350°F. Cream butter and sugars together. Add eggs and pumpkin. Sift together flour, baking powder, salt and baking soda. Add dry ingredients alternately with milk to creamed mixture. Beat 4 minutes with electric mixer at medium speed. Stir in nuts and extract. Pour into three greased and floured 8-inch layer pans. Bake 30 minutes. Cool 10 minutes; remove from pans. Cool completely on wire racks. Spread filling between cake layers and frost top. Garnish with pecan halves, if desired. Chill 2 hours before serving. Yields one 8-inch layer cake.

FILLING:

2 cups milk
1 cup finely chopped pitted dates
2 tablespoons flour

½ cup sugar
2 eggs, slightly beaten
1 cup chopped pecans
2 teaspoons vanilla extract

Combine milk and dates in saucepan; heat to boiling. Combine flour, sugar and eggs; blend until smooth. Add to hot milk mixture. Cook over low heat until thick, stirring constantly. Cool. Stir in nuts and vanilla.

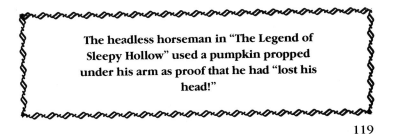

The headless horseman in "The Legend of Sleepy Hollow" used a pumpkin propped under his arm as proof that he had "lost his head!"

"On Golden Pound" Cake with Raspberry Sauce

Delight special-occasion guests with this pumpkin-golden pound cake, its moist richness complemented by a tart-sweet raspberry sauce.

⅔ cup butter, softened	4 eggs
1 cup sugar	2 cups sifted cake flour
¾ cup LIBBY'S Solid Pack Pumpkin	1 teaspoon baking powder
½ to ¾ teaspoon almond extract	⅛ teaspoon salt

Preheat oven to 350°F. In large mixing bowl, cream butter and sugar until light and fluffy. Add pumpkin and extract; mix well. Add eggs, one at a time, beating well after each addition. Add dry ingredients; blend thoroughly at low speed. Pour batter into a greased 9x5-inch metal loaf pan. Gently tap against counter several times to remove any air bubbles. Bake 60 to 65 minutes or until long wooden pick inserted in center comes out clean. Cool 15 minutes. Remove from pan; cool completely on wire rack. Cut into slices. Serve with Raspberry Sauce. Yields 10 to 12 servings.

RASPBERRY SAUCE:

2 packages (10 oz. each) frozen raspberries, thawed	1 tablespoon sugar
½ cup water	2 teaspoons cornstarch
	¼ teaspoon almond extract

Drain raspberries, reserving ½ cup of syrup. Combine reserved syrup with water. In saucepan, combine sugar and cornstarch; mix well. Stir in syrup mixture. Cook over medium heat until mixture boils and thickens. Continue cooking 1 to 2 minutes longer, stirring constantly. Gently stir in berries and almond extract. Chill. Yields about 1½ cups.

Although often treated as vegetables, pumpkins are technically fruit. By one definition, fruit carries and nurtures the seeds that will ultimately become the next generation of the plant.

Creamy Mocha Russe

*This make-ahead dessert flavors pumpkin with creme
de cacao to fill a crumbly-rich chocolate cookie crust.*

2 cups (24) crushed
  chocolate cream-filled
  sandwich cookies
1 cup chopped nuts
¼ cup butter or margarine,
  melted
3 envelopes unflavored
  gelatin
⅔ cup sugar

2½ cups milk
2 cups LIBBY'S Pumpkin Pie
  Mix
½ teaspoon pumpkin pie
  spice
¼ cup creme de cacao
1 teaspoon vanilla extract
2 cups whipping cream,
  whipped

Preheat oven to 350°F. Combine crumbs, nuts and butter; press
into bottom and sides of 9-inch springform pan. Bake 15 minutes.
Cool. In 2½-quart saucepan, combine gelatin and sugar. Stir in
milk. Cook over medium heat until gelatin is dissolved. Add
pumpkin pie mix and spice; continue cooking 5 minutes. Remove
from heat; stir in creme de cacao and vanilla. Refrigerate until
slightly thickened. Fold in whipped cream. Pour into crust. Refrigerate several hours or overnight. Garnish with additional
crushed cookies, if desired. Yields 12 to 14 servings.

Almond Cream Bombe

*Dessert spectacular for special occasions—easy to make
with frozen pound cake and flavorful pumpkin pie mix!*

1 package (16 oz.) frozen
  pound cake, thawed
6 tablespoons almond
  flavored liqueur, divided
3 cups whipping cream
¾ cup sifted powdered sugar
1 cup maraschino cherry
  halves

1 cup LIBBY'S Pumpkin Pie
  Mix
½ cup slivered almonds,
  toasted
½ cup semi-sweet real
  chocolate morsels
1 tablespoon shortening

Cut pound cake into ½ inch slices; cut each slice diagonally in
half. Drizzle cake slices with ¼ cup liqueur. Arrange slices against
bottom and sides of 2-quart mixing bowl lined with plastic wrap.
In large bowl, whip cream and sugar until stiff peaks form. Fold
cherries into 2 cups whipped cream; spread in cake-lined bowl.
Fold pumpkin pie mix into 2 cups whipped cream; spread over
cherry layer. Fold 2 tablespoons liqueur and nuts into remaining
whipped cream; spread over pumpkin layer. Top with remaining
cake slices. Cover; chill several hours or overnight. Unmold on
serving plate. In saucepan, melt chocolate and shortening over
low heat. Drizzle over bombe. Yields 10 to 12 servings.

Party Pleasing Pumpkin Cheesecake

For festive-season guests, make this handsome marbled cheescake, rich with almond liqueur, nestled in a graham cracker-nut crust.

2 packages (8 oz. each) cream cheese, softened
3 eggs, slightly beaten
1 cup sugar, divided
¼ cup almond flavored liqueur
¼ teaspoon salt
1 can (16 oz.) LIBBY'S Solid Pack Pumpkin
1 teaspoon ground cinnamon
½ teaspoon ground nutmeg
Almond Graham Crumb Crust

Preheat oven to 350°F. In large bowl, combine cream cheese, eggs and ¾ cup sugar; mix with electric mixer until well-blended. Add liqueur and salt. Reserve 2 cups mixture. Combine remaining cream cheese mixture with pumpkin, cinnamon, nutmeg and remaining sugar; mix well. Alternate spoonfuls of cream cheese mixture and pumpkin mixture into crust. With knife, gently swirl to marble. Bake 35 to 40 mintes or until cake is almost set (center will still be soft). Cool completely; chill several hours before serving. Yields 10 to 11 servings.

ALMOND GRAHAM CRUMB CRUST:

1½ cups graham cracker crumbs
½ cup ground almonds
⅓ cup sugar
⅓ cup butter or margarine, melted

Combine ingredients; mix well. Press into bottom and sides of 9-inch springform pan.

VARIATION:

Substitute an additional ½ cup graham cracker crumbs for ground nuts.

> Old-fashioned pumpkin is making a place for itself in *nouvelle cuisine*. The chef at a two-star restaurant in Nice, France, serves a delicious filet of sole with sauteed julienne of pumpkin, and a dish in which chicken and little rounds of pumpkin, scooped out with a melon baller, are poached in white wine.

Frosted Pumpkin Creme Log

A perfect company-coming dessert for a holiday meal, tender cake encloses fluffy pumpkin filling, has a whipped cream-nut topping.

FILLING:

1 cup milk
30 (8 oz.) regular-size marshmallows
1 cup LIBBY'S Solid Pack Pumpkin
¼ cup firmly packed brown sugar
1 teaspoon ground cinnamon
1 teaspoon vanilla extract
½ teaspoon salt
3 cups whipped topping, divided
Chopped nuts

In large saucepan, combine milk and marshmallows. Cook over low heat, stirring constantly until marshmallows melt. Add pumpkin, sugar, cinnamon, vanilla and salt; mix well. Cook, stirring constantly, over low heat until slightly thickened, about 5 minutes. Chill until thickened, about 2 hours. Fold in 1 cup whipped topping.

CAKE:

1 cup cake flour
1½ cups plus 2 tablespoons sugar, divided
12 egg whites (1½ cups), room temperature
1½ teaspoons cream of tartar
¼ teasoon salt
1½ teaspoons vanilla extract

Preheat oven to 375°F. In medium bowl, stir together flour and ¾ cup plus 2 tablespoons sugar. Set aside. In large mixer bowl, beat egg whites, cream of tartar and salt until foamy. Gradually add remaining sugar, beating on high speed until meringue holds stiff peaks. Gently fold in vanilla. Sprinkle flour mixture over meringue, folding in gently just until flour disappears. Spread into 15½x10½x1-inch jelly roll pan that has been greased and lined with waxed paper. Bake 15 minutes or until top is light brown. Remove from oven. Cool 10 minutes in pan. Remove from pan. Allow to cool on wire rack, about 1 hour. Invert onto towel dusted with powdered sugar. Remove waxed paper. Starting from narrow end, roll cake in towel. Cool on wire rack. Unroll; spread with cool Pumpkin Filling. Roll; frost with remaining whipped topping. Garnish with chopped nuts. Chill or freeze several hours before serving. Yields 10-12 servings.

Polka Dot Cannoli

Special-day treat: crisp pastry shells contrast perfectly with a creamy, chocolate-dotted filling.

3 cups (1½ pounds) ricotta cheese
1 cup sifted powdered sugar
½ cup LIBBY'S Solid Pack Pumpkin
1 tablespoon vanilla extract

1 cup mini chocolate morsels or finely chopped semi-sweet real chocolate morsels
12 cannoli shells, homemade or packaged

In large mixing bowl, beat ricotta cheese until creamy; gradually add sugar and pumpkin. Beat 2 to 3 minutes. Add vanilla. Stir in chocolate morsels. Chill. Fill a large pastry bag half-full with cheese mixture. Pipe about ⅓ cup mixture into each cannoli shell. Fill shells about 1 hour before serving; chill. Yields 12 servings.

Yesteryear Pumpkin Pudding

The eggs, bread, spices and raisins of traditional bread pudding—plus pumpkin to make it wonderfully new! Microwave if you wish.

8 slices white bread
¾ cup sugar
1 teaspoon ground cinnamon
¼ teaspoon ground nutmeg
2½ cups milk

1 can (16 oz.) LIBBY'S Solid Pack Pumpkin
¾ cup raisins
3 eggs, slightly beaten
½ teaspoon vanilla extract

Preheat oven to 375°F. In large bowl, crumble bread. In separate bowl, combine sugar, cinnamon and nutmeg; mix well. Add remaining ingredients; mix well. Stir into bread. Pour mixture into 2-quart casserole. Set casserole into larger baking pan. Place on oven rack. Fill baking pan with hot water to 1-inch level. Bake 70 minutes or until knife inserted near center comes out clean. Yields 8 servings.

MICROWAVE:

Prepare as directed. Invert a small glass in a 2-quart casserole to form "ring dish." Spoon mixture into dish, surrounding glass. Cook on Medium (50%) 35 to 40 minutes or until pudding begins to pull away from sides of casserole, rotating ½ turn halfway through cooking time.

PUMPKIN QUESTIONS & ANSWERS
QUESTIONS CONSUMERS ASK US . . . AND OUR REPLIES

(Q) Why does Libby produce two types of pumpkin?

(A) Consumers with limited time appreciate the convenience of the ready-to-use Pumpkin Pie Mix which requires only 2 eggs and a small can of evaporated milk to make a pie filling. However, those who prefer to make their pies "from scratch" find Solid Pack Pumpkin and the Libby recipe ideally suited to their families' tastes.

(Q) How long can I store my cans of pumpkin, and where is the best place to keep them?

(A) All canned foods, including pumpkin, are thoroughly heat-processed so they can be stored for extended periods without spoilage as long as the can remains intact. Just as a "rule of thumb," Libby and the National Food Processors Association recommend using canned food supplies within a year of purchase to be assured of maximum quality. Store all canned foods in the coolest cabinet in your kitchen or any cool, dry place. Some folks date cans with a grease pencil or permanent marker as a reminder to rotate supplies.

(Q) What kinds of pastry shells can I use to bake LIBBY'S Pumpkin as a pie?

(A) Our recipe is designed for a homemade pastry or pie crust mix to fit a standard 9-inch pie pan (metal or glass). The pastry is crimped or fluted (by pinching with fingers) to form a high "stand-up" edge. There is also information on our Pumpkin labels for using *regular* or *deep dish* size frozen pie shells for a LIBBY'S Pumpkin pie filling.

(Q) How can I be sure I'm using the 9-inch baking pan the Libby's recipe suggests?

(A) Usually the 9-inch measurement number is shown on the bottom of the pan or dish. You can check your pan or dish by filling it with water. A standard 9-inch pan should hold 4 cups of water.

(Q) Why do my pies sometimes bake unevenly?

(A) If your oven temperature is not accurate or the oven rack you place your pies on is not level, your pies may bake unevenly. Pies should be placed on the middle or lower racks in the oven to prevent over-browning of the top. The top of the oven is always the hottest area.

(Q) My pumpkin pies sometimes crack or pull away from the crust. How can I avoid this?

(A) Positioning your oven rack too close to the top heating unit may cause your pumpkin pie filling to crack as it bakes and to settle slightly on cooling. This may cause the filling to "pull away" from the crust. Another reason for "pulling away" from the crust is over-baking. If this is the case, try reducing your pumpkin pie baking time by 5 to 10 minutes.

(Q) What is the best way to cool my LIBBY'S Pumpkin pies?

(A) Slow cooling is very important for any custard-type pie. As soon as the baked pie is taken from the oven, place it on a wire rack in a draft-free spot. Fast cooling of a custard pie encourages any small cracks, if present, to enlarge and the formation of beads of moisture ("sweating") on the pie's surface.

(Q) How should I store a baked pumpkin pie?

(A) Pumpkin pies are "at their very best" when served the day they're baked. However, if you wish to store pumpkin (or any custard type) pie, refrigeration is necessary. Cover loosely with plastic wrap and refrigerate until serving.

(Q) Can I freeze my pie?

(A) We do not recommend freezing pumpkin (or any custard-type) pie. However, many recipes in LIBBY'S "The Great Pumpkin Cookbook" such as nut bread, muffins, cookies and cake can be frozen. They are ideal "plan-ahead" treats for family and friends.

(Q) How do I store leftover canned pumpkin?

(A) Extra canned pumpkin or pumpkin pie mix can be stored in an airtight plastic or glass container in the refrigerator for up to two weeks. Stir well before using for best results.

(Q) What is the nutritive value of pumpkin?

(A) LIBBY'S Solid Pack Pumpkin and Pumpkin Pie Mix labels display nutrition information. It is also provided on pages 5 and 6 of LIBBY'S "The Great Pumpkin Cookbook."

INDEX